UNRAVELING
GRIEF

**A Mother's Spiritual Journey
of Healing and Discovery**

MEGHAN SMITH BROOKS

UNRAVELING
GRIEF

A Mother's Spiritual Journey
of Healing and Discovery

FOREWORD BY MARIANNE WILLIAMSON

CITIOFBOOKS, INC.
3736 Eubank NE Suite A1
Albuquerque, NM 87111-3579
www.citiofbooks.com
Hotline: 1 (877) 389-2759
Fax: 1 (505) 930-7244

Ordering Information:
Quantity sales. Special discounts are available on quantity purchases by corporations, associations, and others. For details, contact the publisher at the address above.

Printed in the United States of America.

ISBN-13:   Softcover   978-1-962366-87-8
                      eBook   978-1-962366-88-5

Library of Congress Control Number: 2023921305

CONTENTS

"Rev. Meghan held nothing back as she shared the intimate details of the loss of her son in a way that allows you to connect to your own humanity in an empowering, transformative way. Her mastery is she shares it in such a way that you are fed, inspired, deeply connected to spirit and instructed on how you too can come through any trauma or loss in a way that is truly transformational. This is a must read for anyone who has ever experienced loss or trauma and is looking for help with making sense of it while deepening your own spiritual awareness."

~**Rev. Felicia Searcy,** *author of Do Greater Things; Following in Jesus' Footsteps, International speaker and transformational coach*

"Meghan's extraordinary book is profoundly moving, inspiring and transforming. Her personal journey opens up our heart and we experience inside of us an exquisite inner spaciousness. Meghan gifts us spiritual practices not only to heal and integrate our pain but for gratitude and grace to flow into our life."

~ **Imam Jamal Rahman,** *author of The Fragrance of Faith: The Enlightened Heart of Islam, Muslim Sufi minister, teacher, speaker and retreat leader*

DEDICATION

To my heart that resides in the soul of my murdered son, Justin Michael Emmerton, who left his body May 30, 2013. And to all parents who have lost a child, but especially for those who have walked the journey of grief through the loss of a child, or a loved one through violence. May this book offer each of you a way through the experience of grief and the path to rediscovering a meaningful life as you live with grief as a part of who you are in the days, weeks, and years moving forward. All of us who have experienced loss can discover gratitude as a gift hidden within our grief experience and know we are blessed in the process.

ACKNOWLEDGEMENTS

With deep love appreciation I acknowledge my husband, my soul mate, my Anam Cara, Michael, who stood by me all those days and nights as I processed the murder of my youngest son Justin, as I found my way back into my body and the land of the living day by day, year after year.

To my first-born son Ryan, the other half of my mother's heart, whom I am so proud of the accomplishments you have achieved, and way you have navigated through the years of pain and sadness since your younger brother's death. All along you continue to be an extraordinary father to your beautiful daughter, my granddaughter, of whom I am also very proud of and love dearly.

To my mother Suzanne, who has always been there for me offering guidance and support through each challenge in every stage of my life, I am grateful.

To my son Justin's daughter, my first-born granddaughter who will always hold a special place in my heart, wishing for her life journey to be guided by love.

To Reverend Karen Lindvig, Senior Minister of Seattle Unity, my minister mentor and spiritual support since 1993. Someone I admire and look up to as one who walks her talk and flows with the challenges of life demonstrating the spiritual practices she teaches with grace. I will be forever grateful for her guidance and friendship.

I want to especially acknowledge Marianne Williamson for agreeing to write the foreword to my book. I appreciate her support of my grief-healing platform. I am both humbled and deeply grateful for her time and commitment to sharing her insight and recommendation into what this book has to offer. I know her blessing has already made a difference in bringing this message to the world.

To Tom Bird, my publisher and founder of Publish Now, who inspired me to complete my book through his virtual book writing retreat and honored me with a soul read of my book with the words, "Well written, beautifully done, loved your book!" You gave me the confidence to continue the process to bring my book to the public. And to the rest of Tom's team, you blessed me with your professional skills and expertise to make my book become a reality! My gratitude is endless!

I want to honor Rev. Michael Maday, former editor of Unity Publishing and Hay House, now living in the spiritual realm, for his willingness to review and support my book. Though he passed before his words could be revealed, I have been blessed through his receiving my manuscript in ways beyond the physical.

To authors Mary O'Malley, Felicia Searcy, Jamal Rahman and Alden Studebaker for reviewing my book and offering their heartfelt recommendations to the world to read my words. I am humbled by your support and blessing upon this book!

I cannot miss sharing my love and appreciation for my grief healing retreat partner Teri Wilder, who has blessed me with her heart, her wisdom and her vibrational healing as we collaborate in playing together with others, allowing for healing and transformation as a result.

And to the amazingly talented artist Jenny Hahn whose original art was the inspiration for my book cover. Thank you for allowing me to share your creative intuitive gift with the readers of my book!

And finally to my four sisters and all my extended family members, friends, colleagues and ministry members who supported me and walked this journey with me, for you have comforted me beyond measure – another hidden gift within the path of grief

FOREWORD

What you're about to read is a very big book. Not big as in the amount of words, or in the size of the physical product. It's big as in the number of worlds that it traverses. It contains a multitude of dimensions that form the contours of a broken heart.

Meghan Smith Brooks experienced the greatest catastrophe that can befall a human being. Having lived through her son Justin's murder, she made the Herculean effort to process her grief in the deepest way possible. And she succeeded. She succeeded so much in fact that she not only survived, she thrived. And she has turned her grief into extraordinary soul medicine for those whose hearts are breaking as hers has.

I felt tremendous admiration for Meghan as I read the book. How one could find forgiveness, acceptance and gratitude after what she went through is almost unbelievable, yet in reading the book you can tell that she did. She is raw, she is honest, and she is so intent on aligning her will with the will of God even in the most painful places, that she has become a powerful healer of those whose tears she understands so well.

If you are one of those people, I'm glad you found Meghan. And I'm glad you found Justin. For he shines through these pages as much as does his mother, illuminating the greatest mystery of all: that even in death there are the seeds of new life. You could not have found a better guide to lead you through the hour of your agony. Meghan is someone who has been there. She is someone who has found her way through. And in reading this book, I know that you will too.

May all hearts be healed.

— Marianne Williamson

Internationally acclaimed spiritual author, lecturer and political activist with 14 books, four on the #1 New York Times bestseller list, including her first book *A Return To Love*

INTRODUCTION

My Heart Stopped

"When you are sorrowful look again in your heart, and you shall see that in truth you are weeping for that which has been your delight." ~ Kahlil Gibran

The voice within me speaks...

"I am still grieving my son's loss as if it happened yesterday. There isn't a day that goes by I don't think about him, wish I could hear his voice, see his smile, or hold him in my arms… my heart will never stop hurting for his physical presence. My world has been forever changed… A bright part of my life is forever extinguished.

I have come to realize that the grief I feel will never go away, but become something I just learn to live with. There are days that realization makes me angry – that I should not have to learn to live with this loss, I should not have to look at his picture and remember I will never see him in the physical reality ever again. I ache for him every year on his birthday, every Christmas, when I see someone who looks like him, or something that reminds me of him. On the anniversary of his death I am taken back to the day his brother called and said, 'Mom, Justin is gone, they found his body in the river', and my heart stopped…."

Excerpt from the author's statement as read to a defendant in her son's murder case parole hearing April 2018 — used by the State of Missouri National Crime Victims Rights Week (NCVRW) in April, 2019 to assist those who struggle with finding their voice after being impacted by acts of violence and crime.

Many who are reading this may be able to relate to my words. You may be able to put yourself in that place where shocking words spoken by someone else brought you to a place where your world stopped moving and you could not take in another breath .... Or perhaps you have witnessed someone else in that place and did not know how to respond or what to say. Or maybe watched and were grateful you did not have to process the reality of hearing that a son or daughter, husband, wife, partner, or father, mother, sibling or someone you loved was just brutally murdered, or died suddenly by trauma or violence.

No matter what your life reality has been, the pain of loss, and the death of something important in your life, but most especially of a loved one, impacts us and our daily living experience. Grief touches us in many ways and in many forms and it is our role to unravel it in order to embrace it and learn to rediscover a more meaningful life because of it.

My grief experience has become a life lesson that has allowed me to embrace grief and shift into a place of gratitude for everything — *surprisingly.* The following pages invite you to begin breathing again, from wherever you are, and allow the gift of grief to heal, empower, and restore your vitality for living fully.

Have you ever experienced a moment when you felt for sure you may never take another breath? That time stopped and it seemed life has ended? That is what happens when our minds receive something from the world outside ourselves that is more than we can take. Our rational brain cannot process the reality of something we had not anticipated or could ever conceive of in our life experience. It is as if we shut down temporarily for a moment in time so our body can catch up to what our mind is processing. At least that is how I have come to explain what happened to me. I go back to that moment when it felt like my heart stopped, when it felt like I could not take in another breath and reality stood still as I attempted to grasp what I had just heard.

My response was, "Wait, what?" as if I had heard wrong, that could not have been what my son, Ryan, the older of my two sons, on the other end of the line had just said. When he repeated it, those around me noticed I had turned white; that something definitely was wrong. Michael, my best partner ever, and now husband, put his arms around me not even yet knowing what was wrong. In my stunned moment of comprehending the truth of what I had heard, I could not even cry. I went numb. I believe it is our body's defense mechanism to protect us until we are able to process fully. There is a divinely designed system that takes over when we have stopped functioning as we normally would. In hindsight, I can be grateful for that automatic internal-care function or I believe I would have had heart failure.

I know the first 48 hours after receiving those horrendous words, "Mom, Justin is gone, they found his body in a river..." I literally sleepwalked through time. I hardly remember what I did, what was said to me or what happened. I ate when someone said eat, I got dressed when someone said it was time to go out, I made calls but can't remember dialing the phone or what was said. I laid my head down but did not sleep – my mind played over and over again what had happened and tried to answer the question "why?" Eventually I came to accept there is no "why" in murder or in most things that seem to "happen" to us. We cannot rationalize the why, only come to accept the what. But in the first few days and weeks, acceptance is not a place we can arrive.

My heart wrestled with the reality I would never be able to look into my son's beautiful blue eyes or hug him again, and I ached. I still ache. That is something that never seems to go away, even after seven years. It just gets to be more familiar, something I have come to live with even though I will never like how it feels. And there are moments when I want to scream out as much as I did in those first few days … the hurting is so intense. I have to say it really sucks!

I can truly understand why someone would want to bury themselves in addiction to remain numb and never come to terms with the painful reality of death or any other painful life experience, no matter the cause. It is very tempting. But it does not release us from having to deal with the reality and come to terms with it at some point. The thing is, we can never be released from coming to terms with everything life throws at us; it is the reality of living. And if we want to live, we must take steps to move forward and embrace all of life to heal, transform, and be free to create our infinite potential of living life with meaning and purpose. I choose to live – that was the decision I made when I came back from my numb state of existence.

As you read this book, I hope to support you wherever you are on your life path, knowing grief is part of our human experience. We cannot escape grief in our lifetime. My intention is also to offer you hope, belief that you can move forward no matter what experience you have had, to offer you what I have learned, what has been effective, and where I have found relevant spiritual context to understand the value of grief as part of our human existence. I want to unravel this concept of grief, to dissect it and see it for what it is. But also to challenge you to embrace grief as your teacher and commit yourself to practicing the exercises and tools offered throughout this book to help you transform whatever pain and loss you may be experiencing into a meaningful life that demonstrates your heart-felt dreams and ambitions – because you choose to embrace it all and keep moving forward. In the process, I invite you to consciously choose to align with gratitude as a foundational guide to living; and thus rediscover the absolute brilliance of YOU! Become a richer more creative expression of your divine potential because of the life experiences you have been blessed with. And yes, I meant to say, "blessed with," because that is the gift in unraveling and ultimately embracing grief: to know we are blessed because we mourned. We took the time to seek the value of the gift grief may offer.

I have found seeking the Divine Light within can bring comfort and blessing on my journey. This poem by Dr. Sudhir Tongia is one that has blessed me. Please allow it to comfort and bless you on your grief journey as well:

POEM ON THE DIVINE LIGHT

The Divine light is showered on all us,
To dispel negative thoughts, not to curse,
Apathy, anger, hate, lie, ego, and guilt,
All are washed away, for grace to be built.

The Divine Charismatic light impinges to heal
Disease, disorder, disaster, and miserable feel,
All Truth light Nectar, restore inner Bliss,
As Divine Light sparks, souls cross cress.

Divine light propelling Truth Love, has to kindle,
From one soul to soul, for them to mingle,

Far Spread of wave of life in Divinity,
Understanding human to God relation in reality.

The Divine Light energizes all soul humanity,
For growth, grace, and glory via spirituality,
Aspire to become from human to superhuman,
When Divine Blessing is overhead to sustain.

EXERCISE TO BEGIN BREATHING AGAIN:

To support you in times when it feels "your heart has stopped" and breathing is inhibited from the shock of a life event or emotionally charged moment, please practice this exercise to restore deep breathing and the vital life force that brings us back to balance and connection with the wisdom within that guides and sustains us, our Divine Light. * *To listen to the audio link of the following meditation exercise go to website: www.unityawakeningways.org*

- Find a quiet space where you can withdraw from the distractions of the world around you. Turn off your phone or electronics, unless it is soothing, soft instrumental music.

- Sit comfortably in a chair where you can be supported with your back straight and your feet grounded on the floor, hands gently resting on your lap, palms open as if to receive.

- Closing your eyes to the outer reality to open your vision to the inner reality, begin focusing on your breath. See your breath as you breathe in, and breathe out ... following three cycles of breath.

- Now increase the depth of your breathing – allow the inhale breath to expand from your belly as far as you can ... hold for three seconds. Then gently, slowly exhale, releasing all the air as your belly retracts ... hold for three seconds. Breathe deeply for three cycles; inhale & hold three-seconds, exhale & hold three-seconds…

- Return to regular breathing but with an awareness of how your breath is supporting and sustaining your mind, body, and soul connection. Notice how it feels to breath – the difference between shallow and deep breathing. How does it feel different in your body?

- Now set an intention to bring your awareness to your breath whenever you feel it restricted or suspended, and take a deep cleansing breath to bring in the oxygen and energy of life you need to reboot your system. This allows you to be present and ready to listen from within and to hear the wisdom inherently accessible to all beings breathing in this life existence. Remember that our breath is our source breathing us back into each moment. It is so easy to forget how important our breathing is to embrace life and claim all the strength, power and vitality that is ours – especially when a traumatic life event blindsides us without warning. Just BREATHE, breathe, breathe ….

- Bring your awareness back to this now moment and open your eyes, with a renewed sense of awareness of how breathing supports your healing and wholeness.

PART 1

THE BEGINNING OF
THE JOURNEY

CHAPTER 1

LIFE BEFORE

"Life is a journey, it is not where you end up but how you got there"
- Anonymous

"Life is a journey that must be traveled no matter how bad the roads and accommodations."
- Oliver Goldsmith

A spiritual journey always begins long before we realize we have been on one all along. So to understand what had been building as the spiritual foundation to support the most traumatic and pivotal event of my life – the murder of my second-born son – and to understand the ultimate journey through healing and transforming the pain it injected into my heart and consciousness, I must start at the beginning of my relationship with my son, Justin.

When I first discovered I was pregnant with my second child, I was not ecstatic. In fact, I panicked. I was in an abusive marriage with a twenty-month old baby boy and more focused on leaving my relationship to start over on my own then in bringing another child into the world. How could I possibly have another child?

I was already searching for a job to support my baby son and myself at that point – who would hire me now? I felt trapped and didn't know how I would bring another child into a life of what I perceived would be a world of struggle and pain, especially if I were on my own – at least in my naive thinking then.

As I came to accept the reality of another child growing within me, I realized I had to make a new plan. I decided I needed to leave my marriage, even with the prospect of financial challenge and uncertainty. I knew it would be the best move for my health and sanity, and in the long run for my young children, too. After speaking with my parents, they offered me the option of moving in with them temporarily. It was not easy, but I made the move while my husband was out of town at a friend's wedding. I had made a big fuss about not being able to travel because I was pregnant and based on the fact it was an outdoor wedding and the wedding guests all planned on camping. This was totally not my thing under normal circumstances anyway, so it made sense for me not to go. With my father's help, during the small window of time I had, I packed up what was important to me and would be needed for baby Ryan, my first born son, who became a big brother when Justin was born by the end of that year, and moved into my parent's small home across the Puget Sound from Seattle, to Bainbridge Island.

My move set my husband into a rage when he found us gone, as I had anticipated. But I felt I had no other option for my safety. He would not have allowed me to leave with Ryan in tow. His anger scared me and I never knew how volatile his reaction might be. His strategy became to do everything he could think of to manipulate and scare me into coming back. It became a very fearful and turbulent time for me, not knowing how I could possibly manage to get through a seemingly impossible situation. However, courage and perseverance kept me committed to my plan, as I felt safe with a body of water separating us. I needed this time to come to terms with my reality, what was best for my future, and how I would support two little children and myself moving forward. I will always be grateful for my parents unconditionally welcoming the chaos I brought with me into their home during the six months I remained with them.

My husband kept working on me and eventually shifted his strategy, promising to change. Though I was not entirely convinced things would change, I agreed to enter into counseling with him to see if our relationship could be healed for the children's sake – all the while my little Justin was growing within me, waiting to make his entrance into the world. With social services aid, I had found a small one-bedroom apartment near my parents' home so they would be close to help me with Ryan and the new baby, once born. But a month before Justin made his dramatic arrival, I weakened and agreed to allow my husband to move back in with Ryan and me as a family. Fear of being on my own with a newborn and a two-and-a-half-year old became more than I thought I could manage and counseling had convinced me my husband was willing to work on himself. So I caved and we moved into a two-bedroom apartment in the same complex.

Justin came ten days past the doctor's estimated due date, being born "just in time for Christmas," on December 14, 1983. He came quickly. I barely made it to the hospital in time for his birth. My water had broken while putting Ryan to bed, so I called 911, as I was alone at the time. Because I was considered a high-risk pregnancy with Ryan having been breach and born via C-section, I was loaded into an ambulance when it was determined my contractions were already five minutes apart and needed to get to a hospital quickly. Living on Bainbridge Island, which had no hospital, meant I had to get into Seattle to give birth, requiring a thirty-minute ferry ride across the Puget Sound to reach the hospital. Justin was in a hurry to join us, arriving just thirty minutes after I got to University Hospital on the campus of the University of Washington. A second boy – I'm sorry, Justin, I really wanted a little girl as I had grown up with four sisters and loved the idea of all the girl things I had dreamed of sharing with a daughter someday. But there he was, all eight pounds, thirteen ounces of chubbiness!

It was by divine appointment that Justin was a big healthy baby, as his brother Ryan, at two-and-a-half-years old, had determined his baby brother was his personal plaything. If I left the room for a moment, he dumped Justin out of his baby seat from the sofa and would start dragging him under his arms down the hall saying, "*Here's the baby, mama.*" Yes, I was grateful Justin was born resilient and strong or he would surely have experienced more physical distress from the exuberant love of his big brother!

Justin grew up a happy, active, and busy little man. Always smiling, walking at nine months, climbing on whatever he could get on to, and running by the end of his first year of life. I knew I was in trouble the day I found him, having escaped from my sight for an instant, on the kitchen counter, where he had climbed up on a bench so he could get up and reach into the cabinet above and get a packet of instant oatmeal. He had proceeded to open it and dump the entire contents into the glass fishbowl we kept under the cabinet at the end of the counter. He had his little hands in water up to his elbow, mixing the oatmeal … I couldn't believe my eyes that he had managed that in such a short amount of time! He looked at me and said, "*fishes!*" The poor shocked little fish survived, but barely! That was the first demonstration of what living with an adventurous and curious little boy named Justin would be like. I was in for it!At twelve months old, the beginning of my little man's frequent visits to the emergency room began as a result of his fearless nature. On a winter Sunday in December, just after Justin's first birthday, a football Sunday in Seattle, my husband had just left for the Seahawks' game downtown. I thought I might have a moment to relax and made a fresh cup of HOT tea and set it down on an end table in the living room to cool. In the moment it took for me to turn my back, Justin ran across the room and reached right up to grab the hot tea before I could stop him. To my horror I watched as he poured it onto his little baby face and down his left arm. His screams sent me into a panic, but I quickly shifted into "I know what to do" mom mode. I ripped his wet sweatshirt off him and running down the hall to the boy's room, grabbed a sterile diaper (I used cloth diapers from a diaper service) to wrap around the burn on his arm where his sensitive baby skin had already started to melt, and then I called 911. An ambulance arrived and raced us to the Harborview Hospital burn unit emergency center in downtown Seattle. Ryan had the ride of his life, sitting up front with the driver and the siren blaring, oblivious to his brother's pain. I was numb from the emotional trauma watching my sweet little boy passed out with the pain of his burns, his little face flushed and perspiring and occasional tiny whimpers coming from his throat, making my heart cry. It was more than I could possibly bear ... and yet nothing compared to the horror and pain I would experience twenty-eight-and-a-half years later.

We spent two weeks at the burn unit of the hospital, through Christmas. And through it all, Justin's smiley little face remained constant ... except for when the doctors or nurses approached in their green scrub uniforms to take him to the treatment tank, then he would cry and run away from them. I was never allowed in those sessions, as they had to medicate him to handle the pain while scraping away the burned dead skin from the four-inch, third-degree burn on his upper left arm. The tiny quarter-sized burn on his forehead was bandaged, making him look like a soldier home from war, but it healed quickly, more quickly than the deep burn on his arm. He never trusted anyone wearing scrub green again after that traumatic time in his first year of life.

At the end of the second week in hospital residence we were allowed to take Justin home. But I had to continue the treatments in the bathtub, scrapping the dead skin off his burned arm to allow the fresh new skin to come to the surface and prevent a scaly scar from forming. He had to wear a pressure bandage on his arm for a year to keep the scar tissue flat, thus allowing for a smoother healing with a more natural appearance. That scar remained with him for life, a reminder of his first overly adventurous activity – and the first of many emergency room visits I experienced as Justin's mother.

As I kept my weight down chasing after Justin his first few years of life (clearly a bonus I can be grateful for now), I noticed his nature was prone to risk-taking, adventurousness and fearlessly bounding into everything. If he saw something he wanted or something we wanted to do, he would go after it without thinking about the consequences. At age ten, he fell off a slide at the school playground, breaking his left forearm in two places. It was a serious break but did not require surgery, gratefully. He loved having a cast though, as he thought it made him look tough, and that it was really cool because it also doubled as a weapon. Always a boy! And even though the doctor said no bike riding or strenuous activity using his arm for a month, he was off riding his bike the next day anyway. Little dickens he was, rarely listening to or paying attention to boundaries! When I asked how he happened to fall, he said he got pushed off racing to be the first one to the top and then slid down the fastest – and was ecstatic because he won having made it down the fastest, just not down the slide, but off the top of the ladder straight to the ground.

I think deep in my heart I admired his fearless approach to life and secretly wished I could be as bold. There seemed to be a place within me that wanted a sense of freedom to show up in life without hesitancy or fear ... I think my son was my teacher, though I would not realize it until much later, perhaps not until after he was gone.

One of my deepest regrets raising my sons was in not choosing to leave their father earlier, as his abusive ways returned not long after Justin's birth. I tolerated what I could until I realized if I were to be a strong role model and put my sons' health and wholeness first, I had to have the courage to leave the relationship. It had diminished my quality of life to one of fear, physical, mental, and emotional pain, and limitation with his controlling behavior; it was a life of withholding my authentic self and not allowing my heart to be my guide. The occasional physical abuse was painful enough, but the emotional, mental, and sexual abuse had the greatest impact on me. There reaches a point when enough is enough and I had to have the courage to take the risk and leave.

A good friend offered her father-in-law's moving truck, and I took it as a sign to "just do it." One day after my husband left for work, I had gotten Ryan off to school, and dropped Justin off at daycare, I called in sick to my job as a computer programmer (makes me laugh thinking about doing that work back then, it wasn't my passion or enjoyment and eventually I had the courage to leave that behind, too). My friend arrived with others to help me pack everything that I would need for the boys and me to start a new life. I did not allow myself to take anything that had been purchased jointly in my marriage, just taking what was personal and I had brought into the marriage originally, or was specifically for the children. It was enough to start fresh, though I did not have a bed. We stayed with my friend's family for a month. Another friend from work gave me $500 to have some cash to move forward with as I had found myself with zero funds the day after I moved out. My husband had gone to our bank and withdrawn all I had in my personal account, knowing my paycheck had just been deposited, and maxed out my line of credit at our credit union. Because he was a cosigner on the account for emergencies, he could get away with it. He did this while I was at court getting a restraining order … the universe showed up magnanimously in support of my needs though, and the boys and I were just fine despite my husband's deceptive and manipulative actions. When I look back at those days, I see a very strong and courageous woman emerging. It was the beginning of finding myself.

A month later, I found a cute three-bedroom, two-bath manufactured home that I could afford; it was in my friend's neighborhood and our new life officially began. It seemed to be a good new beginning. Little did I know it was really the beginning of a five-year string of legal hearings and a trial that ultimately left me in a financially challenged and emotionally and physically depleted state of mind and body. In hindsight, though, I would not have changed my decision to leave my abusive marriage. I am not sure I would have survived if I hadn't, so it was all worth it.

Eventually the emotional impact of the constant legal, financial, and custody dramas had an impact on the boys as well. Justin went through a very difficult time adjusting to his life of going back and forth from one parent's home to another. His father continuously mentally and emotionally abused his sons by undermining my relationship with them. He encouraged them to act out, to call the police if I attempted to discipline them in any way at all, convinced them they didn't have to listen or mind me, and bribed them with rewards if they reported the trouble they caused back to him. Though I attended weekly counseling sessions with the boys, Justin in particular seemed to have a great sense of pride in refusing to talk or cooperate with the therapist. His father called right before each session to remind them not to cooperate. It was a vicious cycle of mental abuse that generated some very deep anger issues in both boys as they grew into manhood. It was also a very painful time for me as a mother observing actions and behavior I had no control over and the destructive impact it had on the mental health of my young sons as well as myself.

I remember an event during this time when Justin, then a first grader, came home after a visit with his father and went straight into the closet of his bedroom, refusing to come out. He shut down at that point; I could not get him to come out or get him to talk to me. I never knew exactly what triggered his behavior, but I know something had happened on that visit that changed him at the core of his being. Even therapy could not draw it out. That sweet, sensitive little boy became lost to me on some level from that day forward. It was the moment I noticed a profound and permanent shift in him. It saddens my heart even today thinking about it, still wondering what I could have done differently and coming up with the same blank slate.

There reached a point when I did not think I would survive the emotional trauma and mental assault the boys and I were constantly yanked into. I knew the impact on my young sons had reached a limit and the financial drain of therapy and legal issues had taken a toll on my ability to cope, as well. It appeared to me the core issue for my ex-husband was applying pressure to disrupt my life and intimidate me into giving up any request for child support. So I made the most difficult decision of my life up to then, to give up physical custody of my sons. I believed by doing that, the mental and emotional stress they had endured for so long would be relieved, as their father would believe he had won. My love for them was greater than playing his game. There was no evidence of physical abuse toward them, so my hope was that the mental and emotional abuse would cease and desist once he felt he was in control. We negotiated a plan and I held an intentional prayer for it to be honored.

The decision to allow my sons to live primarily with their father sent me into an emotional tailspin of living in a world of not having my loud, feisty boys in my day-by-day life. I must be honest and admit I thought about ending my life to avoid living with the pain of that life-changing decision. I felt remorse, guilt, and extreme sadness, constantly questioning whether I had done the right thing. During that time I made friends with a wonderful woman from my church who had gone through a similar situation. She became my stronghold to encourage me to stay focused on loving my boys the best way I could and to remember to let them know that every chance I got. I never knew the demons that haunted her at the time as I was so caught up in my own pain. But she kept me from choosing to end my life. Ironically several months later she ended hers. I was shocked, as I never knew her struggles. She kept me grounded and I thought she was just as strong for herself. I realized how important life was and I would never want to bring that level of pain into my young sons' lives after that. Her final gift to me, her legacy I used to enhance my life, was in choosing to be there for my sons even when it was really difficult.

It was shortly after that I experienced a spiritually inspired dream that gave me the courage to keep going, knowing I had made the right decision for both the boys and myself at the time. As I was experiencing a lot of internal fear and self-doubt, I believe my divine self was offering me the comfort and support I needed to courageously face my future and listen to my inner voice. The guilt and shame I felt for giving away the physical custody of my boys had been eating away at my self-confidence and taking a toll on my personal demeanor and outer expression. I was depressed and unsure of what to do with myself, and fearful my sons would think I didn't care about them. Even though I reminded them how much I loved them every chance I got, I knew at their ages of eight and ten they would not be able to fully understand what I had been going through or the cause of the decision I made.

In the dream, I found myself with my sons in a small cottage in the woods. We were happy but felt a dark presence creeping up around our home. We became very fearful and frightened as the presence peered into our windows, with scary eyes. It felt as if we could not escape its overwhelming dark energy. We hid under the dining room table hoping it would not see us. It was then that I realized if I did not have the courage to open the door and face it, we would be overpowered as it took over our lives. I was terrified but at the same time was compelled to stand up to whatever it was outside our home, our safe place.

I opened the door and walked outside. The darkness consumed everything, taunting me to step toward it. As I did it took the form of Darth Vader. (Star Wars was prominent in movie theaters at that time and a big favorite of the boys, so I believe was an influence in my mind). The frightening, huge figure of darkness stood before me, daring me to approach and come closer. Somewhere inside I knew I had to face this fear, and at the same time "knew" I would not be destroyed. As I stepped closer a dark bottomless pit formed in front of the Darth Vader figure and I knew if I stepped any further I would fall in, to be forever consumed with the poisonous darkness and be separated from my children for eternity.

But just as I took that last step – knowing I had no choice – my eyes were drawn to a light over the shoulder of the dark force and it became radiant as it beamed into my heart. It said within me, "Do not be afraid, stay focused on this divine light and let it guide you forward. You will not be harmed if you keep your focus on the light as you step forward." Despite my fear, a peace came over me and I stepped into the appearance of the dark pit. As I did, a beautiful bridge appeared for me to walk over the pit and into the most glorious garden one could ever imagine. And the Darth Vader figure began to shrink and fade away into nothing, its dark energy no longer having power over me. I realized what I feared was an illusion and the light held everything that was true.

I continued on the path of light before me to where I found a bench inviting me to sit among the fragrant roses and flowers of the garden. I felt at peace and happy and knew I was where I belonged. Then my thoughts went to my children, where were they? Were they safe? The voice within the light assured me they were safe and well. They would be free to join me in time, but my job now was to focus on healing my heart and reestablishing my life purpose. As I had the courage and the faith to grow and develop my spiritual nature, I would be guided to be a loving presence in my sons' lives and know when to step in as I was needed. I had no need to fear the future or what it may bring. My children and I will always have a heart connection, one that can never be broken. That gave me the faith and the courage to go on.

I awoke, feeling the peace in my heart that my sons were safe and well wherever they were and I would continue to be a loving presence in their life in the right way and at the right time. It wasn't something that instantly changed my reality, but it planted seeds I was able to begin implementing as I became more aware of that inner guidance system working on my behalf. I began to become more aware of who I knew deep in my heart I was meant to be. I had turned the corner of wanting to leave the life I had and instead focused on creating the life I wanted to live. I continue to take myself back to that garden, surrounded by the divine light of life – what I know is the source of my inner power within me (that which may be called God) – and allow it to guide and love me whenever I feel overwhelmed or challenged. It has been a life-long gift of Spirit. It is what helped to sustain me in more challenging life events many years later, but also in making peace with the decision I made to allow my sons to live primarily with their father for the time being.

CHAPTER 2

CHAOTIC TEEN YEARS

"Be grateful for all the obstacles in your life. They have strengthened you as you continue with your journey."
~ Anonymous

When Justin was thirteen, and his brother fifteen, their father decided to take a job transfer to England and convinced the boys it would be a fun and adventurous time to move with him for the three-year contractual period. I panicked over the idea, knowing it was an underlying ploy to get them away from me and have a stronger influence over them. Because I wanted to do the right thing by them, I requested the court to appoint a guardian ad litem, as I knew I would not be able to negotiate a plan on my own. She met with all of us independently and evaluated what would be in the boy's best interest. In the end I realized my sons would not be able to understand the emotional trick being played on them and I would be the "bad guy" in the situation if I prevented them from going to England. So I then asked the guardian to assist in writing a parenting plan that would honor my rights and not allow their father to separate and isolate the boys from having a healthy and involved relationship with me while they were in England. Their father quickly agreed to the terms, too quickly. I realize in hindsight that he never really had intended on following the plan, knowing that once he and the boys were out of the country it would be hard to enforce. He proceeded to immediately move forward with their exit from the United States before I could get any information on an exact date or time, or destination information, they left, just before Easter, 1997.

I was allowed a couple of days together with my boys before they were to leave for England. We spent special time talking about what it would be like to live in a foreign country and how we could stay in contact. I knew there would be some travel days I may not be able to communicate with them, but had anticipated being provided with their new address and a phone number so we could stay in touch. I shared with my sons how even by living in different time zones we could share a connection of the heart and spirit. I had special little metal angel pocket charms I gave to each of them to carry in their pockets as a reminder they were loved. The boys and I blessed them together on our last night before they left. I also gave them each a small white candle to take with them to light each night, even though night would be at different times for us, and I would also light one each night for them as we sent each other love and prayers before we went to sleep every night we were apart. It was my attempt at introducing spirituality and ritual with meaning and intention into their lives, and a way to assist each of us in feeling connected even though ocean's apart. They seemed to understand and respond to the idea. It made for a very heartfelt goodbye time for us, one I am forever grateful for having had. Later, they each shared how it had been very special for them in adjusting to their new life in a foreign reality away from everything they ever knew. And for me, I felt a heart connection with my sons that carried me through some very tear-filled nights.

The reality I had expected when they left was not what happened. I was not provided an arrival date or time or a contact phone number or address, or allowed to go to the airport to say goodbye to my sons. It happened too quickly to have the court intervene on my behalf, which was their father's plan. I was just notified they were leaving early the next day after they left my home and it was suggested that it would be too traumatic for the boys if I came to the airport. Boom, that was it. It was the beginning of a long and painful separation that did not follow the court agreement. I did not receive my first phone call from my sons in England for more than three weeks, and I still was not provided a contact to call them from my end, being told they were not in permanent living circumstance yet. Every call was monitored by their father to prevent them from sharing many details of their new life, or to express their feelings about their new environment or new school. I did not know then how emotionally and mentally impairing this time was for Justin, in particular. It had a lifelong impact on him that I realize in looking back on those years, began the road to his choices in the future that eventually led to the connections with those who would be responsible for the end of his life.

He was allowed to return to my home for the summer, as agreed, but it was a hard fight to make even that happen. At sixteen, Ryan had chosen to stay in England that summer after being bribed to have a friend come and travel with him for a month throughout Europe instead of coming to visit me. That was something common in Europe for teens to do, but not common for teens from the United States, so I was a bit concerned about their safety and their knowledge of how to navigate around foreign countries on their own. However, I couldn't compete with the excitement that opportunity offered. It ended up being a great adventure for Ryan and he grew tremendously during that experience. So that was a good outcome from a period of time that was most challenging in almost every other way, especially for Justin and me.

When Justin arrived home from England, the first thing he did was get down on his knees by his bed and cry, holding his beloved dog Dudley, a little terrier/Shih Tzu mix we had adopted from the pound at Justin's pleading years before. It broke my heart to see the pent-up emotion he had been holding back. It came out that he was not allowed to reveal his feelings or share any of his dislike for living in England. He had not adjusted well at all, especially with the school system at the private boys' school they had been enrolled in. Justin had a hard time with school before leaving, so the foreign school system in England was even more challenging. I believe he was dyslexic and perhaps had other learning challenges that the emotional abuse in his life deepened. Therefore with the lack of understanding or support in his English school, he did not thrive.

I came to find out he had been teased and abused by the boys at his English school because he was not at the level they were in many subjects – like French, which he had never taken, and they were already speaking fluently, having been taught as part of the regular curriculum since the English version of kindergarten. He had shut down in many ways during that four months away from his home in the United States. This was another emotional setback in life that contributed to the adult he became and how he struggled to find his way.

That summer we took a trip to Victoria, B.C., on Vancouver Island, a four-hour ferry ride from Anacortes, WA, just north of Seattle. My second husband, whom I married when the boys were ten and twelve, had access to a rustic little cabin outside of Victoria that had been in his family for generations. No one was using it that summer so it was available for me to take Justin, along with one of his best friends and of course Dudley, for a ten-day getaway.

I am so grateful I have this cherished memory of time with Justin from that summer. It was a time he was still okay with going away and hanging out with his mother – made acceptable because he had a friend to be with at the same time and Dudley to offer additional companionship and adventure.

The cabin had electricity and indoor plumbing, a small basic kitchen, but no Internet, cable, or good cell service. Of course it was also before every teen had a cell phone and the Internet was not yet a required function of life. We had a radio and a video cassette player (no DVD!) to watch movies, a covered porch with a big table to play games and put puzzles together, with a lantern for light at night. The boys slept in a separate sleeping bungalow, which at thirteen they thought was the coolest part of the whole experience! It was like camping out with some conveniences and a solid roof over our heads. The cabin sat on a bluff above the Puget Sound ocean waters of the Vancouver Island Inlet. Surrounded by tall fir trees but with a view of the beach, it was truly a special little getaway place. Good thing we were all in good physical shape, as it also had a very steep winding stair climb down to and back up from the beach.

We spent our days hanging out at the beach, my personal version of paradise. I would pack a lunch and snacks, bring a blanket and towels to make our beach day camp. We collected shells, splashed in the cool water, walked for miles and watched Dudley attempt to dig up Gooey Ducks, even catching one or two in the process – an amazing feat! Gooey Ducks are large clams with 4-8 inch shells, really thick, long necks and super-fast diggers. Their necks stick out from the sand about an inch or so and spout water when you walk near them – often spraying up your legs. To catch them you have to grab their necks quickly and start digging with hands or shovel as fast as you can to get to the shell before it goes too deep. They have been known to stretch their necks out for several feet, often causing their necks to break away from their shells to get away, so you have to be strong and fast! The fact that Dudley caught one was a demonstration of his stupendous digging skills. Of course he also ended up covered in sand from head to toe and needed daily hosing off to come into the cabin. He clearly did not care, as he was having the best time of his dog life.

The boys had the time of their lives, too. They built forts with driftwood and played boy games while I sat and read in the sun taking in the salty smell of the air and the relaxing sound of the ocean waves. We went into the little village nearby to explore, pick up an occasional meal and groceries – as I cooked most of our meals at the cabin. Our evenings were especially meaningful, as we spent our time sitting on the outdoor porch with the lantern light, eating a simple meal and playing cards, board games, putting puzzles together, or watching movies. We made popcorn and cookies, laughed and talked about life from their thirteen-year-old world-reality, which provided me some interesting insight. I could have stayed there forever, even with apartment-sized appliances and little space in which to function. The ferry rides to and from were part of the wonderful adventure, too. We were blessed with an Orca whale pod swimming near us on the way home and bald eagle sightings on the way up! I will always be glad we had that special time together, mother and son. It seemed to also be a time Justin was able to put his painful thoughts and feelings aside and remember to be the boy he still was – for a short period of time.

At the end of the summer when it was time for Justin to return to England, he refused to go back. That was putting me in the position of having to either ask the court to change the parenting agreement, which would have been an uphill challenge, or be in violation of the current agreement. When Justin asked his father to allow him to stay with me in the United States, he emphatically refused, no surprise. I became as desperate as Justin to find a way for him to stay where he felt safe and happy, where he could be with his friends, attend the school he knew and where it was familiar to him rather than foreign. It had become obvious to me Justin did not fit into the life in England, whereas his brother seemed to have the personality and extra years of maturity that allowed him to integrate into the foreign lifestyle and find a way to fit in.

So Justin took it into his own hands. Behind my back, he plotted for a way to not get on the plane back to England. He was determined to stay in the only place he really knew, and with his maternal grandmother's help, his plan came together. Apparently, as I found out much later, Justin's plan was to escape from the airport when I took him on the day of his flight. He planned to disappear after going to the restroom before arriving at the gate for boarding, then exiting without me seeing him, going down to the transportation level of the airport, taking a bus to downtown Seattle, and ultimately get down to the ferry docks. He somehow managed to pull all that off with his sheer wit and determination, and planning from his cohort, who I discovered later to be my mother. I unknowingly contributed by providing him with some cash for his travel. Once he reached the ferry docks, he took the thirty-minute ferry to where my mother met him on the other side. They proceeded to drive up the peninsula to a cabin a friend of my mother's owned, planning to camp out for as long as necessary to keep Justin safe and where he would not be found until the next part of the plan could be implemented.

I, of course, was frantic when I could not find him at the airport, but based on his behavior and determination to stay, I had an intuitive feeling he was fine, that he had made his escape, most likely with help from others. He was very resourceful in his persistent way; that had been his personality since he learned to walk. I contacted airport security and they made a report and had his description sent to all security exits to watch if he showed up. They were concerned he may have been kidnapped at first, though I knew Justin would fight off anyone who attempted to nab him and cause a scene, so it seemed unlikely that had happened. The plane to New York where he would have changed planes to London left without him. I eventually went home to wait to see if Justin would contact me. I was frightened for him, but again, somehow knew in my heart that he was both fearless and courageous and most likely doing better than I was – I had to believe that. When he was determined to do something, nothing got in his way. This was one of those times I just knew he had been successful in achieving his goal, at least for the moment.

Though I was threatened with jail if I did not produce Justin and get him on the next flight to England, I could not provide something I had no knowledge of. I had no information where he was or where to find him, and because the police could not prove otherwise, I was not arrested. Justin held out in his hiding place with my mother while my parents requested temporary custody of him to keep him safe and allow time to resolve the parenting plan. That was when I was included in what had been their ultimate plan and felt a deep sense of relief and hope. The court order was eventually approved, so Justin returned with his grandmother to his grandparent's home in the Kingston, WA area (across Puget Sound from Seattle) for the temporary period of time granted.

The court order allowed both his father and me to call him at his grandparents' home – but I was not allowed to see him, as his father's attorney argued it would be an unfair advantage for me to see him, when his father, being in another country, could not. He also had to start a new school, as his grandparents lived in a different city and county and the distance prevented him from rejoining his friends at the school he attended before leaving for England the previous year. This was another level of pain generated in the life circumstances of my sweet little boy born just in time for Christmas…

The calls from his father became very abusive, threatening him to return to England and forcing him to choose between his father and me, as he would not be allowed to have both of us in his life after that point. Justin would break down in tears after each call and share the disturbing comments his father had said with both his grandmother and myself, as he called me after each conversation for comfort and reassurance. He was very traumatized by the cruelty of what he was experiencing with those calls. When Justin told his father he was recording the conversations, even though he was just using it as a threat at that point, his father shouted back that he was, too. My attorney informed us that automatically gave legal authority to record future calls, as it was a form of permission. My mother was able to assist Justin in recording some of the most abusive and threatening calls that came almost daily. Those calls left him sobbing and breaking both my mother's heart and mine, but truly shattered Justin as well. It was horrible not being able to comfort him during those terrible months.

Once those recordings were shared with his father's attorney, I was given immediate custody; they knew there was no contest when this abuse was revealed. Justin was allowed to both stay in the United States, and return home to live with me. The sad and painful consequence from that decision was that Justin had to choose me over his father; therefore his father told him he no longer had a father. Justin never shared how he really felt about that, though I knew it was a painful burden on him. He kept things tight within, so I did not know the level of pain he felt. But I believe it affected him very deeply and influenced his more daredevil life choices after that point. He seemed to not care what happened to him physically or legally, and consequences did not matter.

As Justin had been forced to start another school while living with his grandparents, he now had to start over yet again mid-school year. And even though he was back to his original school and friends, nearly a year had passed since he last attended, so he was not in sync with the curriculum being taught at that point. All of those adjustments took a high toll on his sensitive nature and academic success. Though he wanted the world to believe he was tough, internally he was a very sensitive soul who loved animals and had little tolerance for injustice. During this time he became more vulnerable with me both in confiding his fears, his struggles, and the horrors of his time in England. Though I discovered many years later, he did not reveal the sexual abuse by the private school boys, the most significant reason for his not wanting to return to England. He needed to feel loved, protected, and free to be who he was. He frequently wanted me to pray with him before bed and sit with him quietly. For a brief time he allowed me in, but sadly it did not last long.

Soon I noticed his behavior changing. He began drinking and smoking behind my back, and hanging with the other boys at school who were not motivated to learn or follow rules. As his behavior changed he shut down his sensitive side to show an outer toughness in which he would stand courageously, no matter what the threat. He did join the wrestling team during that eighth grade year of middle school and excelled in that sport. He did not take losing lightly and would fight to win no matter how tough his opponent was. He was quite the scrambler. It was the persona he showed up in how he approached the world at that point; no one would hold him back or take advantage of him.

He was fearless in all things, even in confronting the law. As he moved into his freshman year of high school, he began getting into trouble doing pranks with his friends like throwing eggs at a house, vandalizing for fun, and tormenting the neighbor's horses, even though he loved animals. When sent to juvenile detention, he would beg me to get him out to come home, but refused to let anyone else see him as weak or vulnerable. He would do what he was told to get out of the consequences but had no plans of following up with what was expected in the long run. He struggled in school because he did not read well and felt stupid and unworthy, only causing him to act out more. I did not realize how much he had been lying to me at that time, but in hindsight it was obvious. A mother always wants to believe the best on some level, we are vulnerable that way. And I was no exception....

His resistance to following any of my house rules and with his behavior becoming destructive on many levels, became a daily torment in my life. As a result, I also shut down emotionally, feeling like he was out of control and I had no power to change what was happening. He would break furniture if he couldn't have his way; punch holes in the wall; not honor curfews; and refuse to get up for school. I began seeing a therapist and when I could convince Justin to join me, he begrudgingly would come, though it did not seem to generate the changes I hoped for. He resisted cooperation, a holdover from the brainwashing of his early childhood.

His brother was still in England at this time, and I knew Justin really missed him. I thought perhaps that contributed to his acting out, but it was much deeper. I was really barely functioning by this point, so that did not help Justin in his troubled world. The mental and emotional abuse we had both suffered was playing out in our lives in painful and destructive ways. His stepfather traveled for work most of every week, so I was mostly on my own and did not have the emotional support I needed. I began withdrawing from participation in life and not caring for myself in ways that would have given me the greater mental and physical energy I desperately needed. I knew Justin was reacting to his internal pain and had no understanding – or skill – to process or transform on his own. And I also knew I did not have the ability or skill to support him in processing it when he was so resistant to accepting help on any level from anyone.

Ryan insisted on returning to the United States for his senior year of high school to be with his friends and play American football. He was able to make that happen, though was not allowed to live with me when he returned. Instead of coming home to me, it was arranged for Ryan to live at his father's U.S. residence with his father's life-partner who had not moved full time to England. Because their father still harbored anger toward me over Justin's refusal to return to England, and was legally given permission to stay with me, his father was adamant about Ryan not living with me. Ryan spent most of his time at our house anyway; just going home to his father's to sleep, to satisfy his father's rule. It helped Justin to have his brother back, but by then the road he was sliding down had dug a hole too deep to change without serious intervention. That was something I was not prepared to manage with the limited resources I had available to me, though I continued to seek help wherever I could. When a child becomes a teenager, it becomes much more difficult to gain their acceptance or agreement in showing up for such things as therapy or group support, or implementing consequences for their actions. I felt trapped and helpless.

Many years and deeper addictive behavior became Justin's world. He never completed high school. After his freshman year it became too difficult to get him to show up and the school system eventually shut the door on him. We tried an alternative high school, but even that became a dead end when he refused to attend regularly. I have lived with the guilt of not being an effective mother around that for too long. I still do not know what I could have done to change the direction of his life, as once a child attains a certain age, they are their own person and living with their own choices, consequences, and results. I have had many years of therapy around those feeling of helplessness in the throngs of mental and emotional abuse over extended periods of time. This has helped me to realize I may have had different results had I had the tools to process the events and situations in my life more effectively. But at the time I had not been taught or even made aware of some of the things I now know. Perhaps they will serve me as a grandmother and in supporting my surviving son now, but I can only be supportive and offer advice as it is welcomed.

CHAPTER 3

LAST DECADE; EMERGING PATHS

"It is not in the stars to hold our destiny but in ourselves."
~ William Shakespeare

"The only person you are destined to become is the person you
decide to be."
~ Ralph Waldo Emerson

Somewhere along the way, I began to tap back into listening to that tiny little voice within me that said "Change, take back your life, do what your passion calls you to do, go back to your garden and listen…" I began a spiritual path to awareness that no matter what I had experienced, I could transform the hurt, angry, unforgiving, painful, and grieving part of myself and create something different, better, creative, and abundant. I resumed my spiritual search for myself from which I had stumbled off the path, and returned to attending Seattle Unity Church with a more intentional focus. My mother encouraged me to honor this call within me, and for that I am grateful. It was a place I could learn, grow, heal, and transform the person I thought I was, and take a deeper step into becoming who I know I am now.

Eventually I saw that the teacher in me wanted to emerge and followed a path to meet the educational credentials to become a Licensed Unity Teacher with the Unity organization. I began taking spiritual courses on meditation, metaphysics, spiritual teachings and prosperity at my spiritual center that gave me the courage and strength to stay focused on what I wanted to make of my life. I eventually completed all the required courses to graduate from the Continuing Education Program of The Unity School of Christianity, now dba Unity Worldwide Spiritual Institute, and became an official Licensed Unity Teacher in 1995. This designation provided me with the credentials to offer adult education courses for credit through the spiritual center I was affiliated with as offered by The Unity School of Christianity. At that time I began teaching through Seattle Unity Church. With that accreditation, I found the courage to step out and participate in life in new and rewarding ways, teaching, speaking, and officiating weddings around the Pacific Northwest. My sons, I think, were proud of me for doing something that made me a happier, better, more compassionate, and healthy person. Though they did not fully understand my path, they came to some of the services when I was a speaker and supported me in my new work.

While I was near the end of my course work I had another powerful dream that again transformed my understanding of life and my role in it. During a particularly restless period of juggling my courses and being an active part of my sons' lives, despite the challenge of working through their father's controlling my every activity with them, I had a very vivid dream that gave me inspiration and insight about the purpose of life. It has served me to this day as a reminder of the spiritual core that is the creative energy driving all life. The dream had such an impact on me that I had wished I might experience it again as I wanted to make sure I really got it, that I really understood the message that seemed very clearly meant for me.

The next night I had the very same dream, but I realized it was more of an experience. It was exactly the same and it felt as if I had been taken somewhere. I know that seems unbelievable, maybe even strange, but on some level I am convinced I really had an out-of-body experience at night to be given important information to apply to my life. In the dream I was in a place unlike Earth, more like a dream reality of "heaven," with misty clouds as carpets moving slightly up to create transparent walls. I could see a group of people beyond me calling my name, and I remember thinking "How do they know me?" They came up to greet me enthusiastically saying, "It's your turn, it's your turn!" They were jumping up and down as if this was something to be really excited about. When I asked, "My turn for what?" one of them explained. I was told it was my turn to play the Game of Life. I liked to play games and thought it could be fun. I asked, "What do I have to do?" Another person said, "First you roll the dice to see how long you have to play the game. Then you choose a life purpose card to see what you will be focusing on in the game. Finally you choose who you want to be your parents that are already in play in the game and then who you want to join you in support of achieving success in your game." I thought that sounded interesting. I did not ask how that all was supposed to work, but I did ask, "How do you begin playing?" I was informed that the game was played on a planet called Earth and I would be born into the game through my parents, arriving as an infant. I would need to grow into my life to work on my plan to experience my purpose.

Then they shared something very important for me to know, that once you are born into the game, you will lose all memory of playing a game, what your purpose is, how long you have to achieve your purpose, and that you chose your parents or remember anyone you chose to join you in the game. I recall thinking, *That doesn't seem fair...* But it was explained, "You do have one very special option to receive clues along the way, provided by God, our universal parent and creator of this Game of Life. The clues are available only when you remain aware in each moment and listen to the voice within offering the clues. You will not hear the clues if you get caught up in living in past experiences or anxious about what the future will bring or fearful about life in general. Only in the present moment, listening within, will you receive guidance to support your efforts of playing the Game of Life successfully. Your game will end when you achieve your purpose. You may then choose to leave the planet or you may remain to support others in their game's success."

I was amazed this all came to me. I woke up immediately in the middle of the night and wrote down everything I experienced so I could capture it to use as a blueprint for life starting then. It all made sense in a very playful way. I considered why I may have been given this information in that form, and the realization came to me that I had become way too serious about life and had stopped enjoying my reality. I needed to be shaken up a bit and reminded that life was supposed to be enjoyed; that I deserved happiness and success. I had the potential to discover my true calling if I started listening to the voice within me and had the courage to follow it. This dream gave me the encouragement and the excitement to consider what my true-life purpose was and what changes I needed to make both within me and around me to move in the direction of success, using the newly acquired credentials I was on the verge of receiving to lead the way.

I had begun to tap into my creative side again, that part of myself I had let die for so long, and consider what I really wanted to do with my life. I also was preparing for my most challenging and painful time of my life without knowing it, setting a foundation to support my survival of one of the most excruciating experience's anyone could ever live through, the murder of my sweet little second-born child who came into this world just in time for Christmas.

After ten years teaching, speaking, officiating weddings and memorials, and leading a small spiritual community for two of those years, I answered the call to apply to Unity Institute, a private seminary now called Unity Worldwide Spiritual Institute, to become an ordained Unity minister. Through many trials and tribulations, as they say, I was accepted into the two-year residence program beginning in July of 2005.

Several years before that, when he was eighteen, Justin had been diagnosed with Non-Hodgkin's Lymphoma. He went through four of six recommended sessions of chemotherapy, but refused to follow his doctor's advice and complete the final two. Another example of his stubborn tenacity was in refusing to complete the recommended treatments, as he didn't like the way they made him feel. I am sure anyone in his position would have felt the same, but would not have risked going against doctor recommendations. His doctor was surprised four treatments seemed to be enough, when his body went into remission. I think it was an example of his determination and refusal to let anything beat him. Justin accepted he was cancer-free and moved forward without looking back. I found it a profound example of holding positive intentions for his body's cells to renew and heal and demonstrate the manifested results. This was a lesson I could use in future life challenges.

Justin had yet to find himself at this point in life, not that all nineteen-year-olds had, but I believe he was fearful of holding a vision for his life because he did not know if he had a future – the cancer might come back. It did, however, create a space where he lived in the moment responding to life as it happened and not holding back from whatever he wanted to do. He did not realize he was practicing a spiritual principal of awareness; being in the state of noticing in the present moment and choosing from that point of awareness rather than past repetition or future uncertainty. Though he had not allowed himself to choose big goals, he did choose to face things many fear, like skydiving, because the opportunity presented itself, so he said "yes!" He relished doing the dangerous and outrageous, living on the edge, but perhaps without the filter that might have been beneficial on some level. He lived in the moment but not in the full state of awareness of the wisdom to guide him.

When I was preparing to move from the Northwest to Unity Village, Missouri, outside of Kansas City, to begin my ministerial training, Justin decided he wanted to move there with me. He was ready for a change and the adventure of something different. But I also think he did not want to be so far away from me, his only real link to someone who loved him unconditionally and accepted him no matter what foolish or outrageous things he did – at least my mother's heart wanted to believe that!

So we made plans and joined with another Seattle friend who had been accepted into the same ministerial class at Unity seminary with me, and we began a caravan across country. Justin had gone to Montana for a while to work and was living with his grandmother, the same one who helped save him from returning to England, so he met up with us along I-90 in Missoula. We spent the next three days, each in our own car, driving through many beautiful places in the Northwest, through mountains, into the plains of Montana, and the dry barren nothingness of South Dakota, stopping for a side trip to see Mount Rushmore. Justin was thrilled to see this historical site, and now I am so grateful we took the time to share that experience together. It is one of the gifts I hold in my memory bank with him. Something I learned from that experience is to attempt to remember to say "yes" when presented with an unexpected opportunity rather than live in regret of the lost moment in time. That was one of them.

We eventually arrived at Unity Village outside of Lee's Summit, MO, our new home. I helped Justin find a small rental apartment with his commitment of finding a job within thirty days to pay his own expenses. He quickly found one at Toy's R Us in the warehouse, which he loved because he got to drive a forklift! Soon two of his best childhood friends joined him and he seemed happy in this new adventure of his life. Justin was a very outgoing and friendly young man, so he easily made friends and forged strong, life-long bonds. Those two friends continue to remain part of his older brother's "tribe" and of the group of boys who call me "mom" to this day.

I began my challenge of studying, completing, graduating, and becoming ordained while we got together at least once a week to stay connected. It was a growing time for us both. Justin also met someone who became the love of his life during that time at Toys R Us, and the woman who would become the mother of his child, my first granddaughter, born September 24, 2007, three months after my graduation and ordination from Unity Institute.

Much to my sadness, Justin's alcohol and drug addiction became more prevalent during this time, as well. I was called to the emergency room on more than one occasion for his overdosing, sometimes intentionally, as he struggled with the demons of his short life, unresolved anger, unforgiveness, emotional pain, and the grief of not having the father he wished for.... For from the time he chose to stay with me instead of returning to England, and his father's forced choice to either have a father or a mother, Justin had periodically tested the waters to see if anything had changed. At this point, while in Missouri, he still did not have a relationship with his father, just an occasional phone call when he would hear on the other end of the line, "Did you change your mind?" and if he said no, which he had continued to say, then his father would respond, "Then you don't have a father...." It devastated Justin. Though he would not ever verbalize it, he chose to act it out instead. I think the little boy in him never gave up hope the father he called would be a different person on the other end of the line. His stubbornness would not allow him to share what he truly felt, so he drowned it in addictions.

He also broke his hand on numerous occasions, beating the wall from his unresolved anger. I believe his right hand had permanent damage at some point from the beatings it took. And still he refused help. With all my spiritual counseling training and new ministerial education, I could not reach him. I struggled with that too. I learned in a very personal and challenging way that no one changes unless they want to, or want to realize a benefit to change. Justin had not reached that point yet. Though I never gave up on him.

Because of his chemo treatments, he believed he could never father a child, so when his girlfriend became pregnant, he was ecstatic! I think the little boy in him that never really grew up felt his child would allow him a childhood he never got to fully realize. He loved to have fun, do playful things, go on wild adventures and participate in exciting activities, and now he could do it with his child. Though he was not emotionally mature or ready to be a father, he was going to become one anyway. Finances were a constant struggle for Justin, as his jobs were not always stable, so I was manipulated into helping at times when I was not really in the position to do so. It also contributed to a volatile relationship with him on and off; our integrity and moral views of life were not in sync.

One of my deepest and cherished memories came at Christmas, 2006. I was six months from graduating from seminary and hopefully being accepted to be ordained the following June. My father had been on a feeding tube for eighteen months after having had a series of strokes that left him unable to swallow most food, so was on a mostly liquid diet. I knew with his health deteriorating, Christmas would be an important time to make the effort to go to Montana for a visit. I was living on a student's very limited income, but found a way to not only get myself to Eureka, Montana, but also to have Justin fly back with me to spend Christmas with his grandparents and some extended family. Something in me told me it was important to share this trip with Justin and have this special time with my father, and I am eternally grateful I listened to that inner voice.

Justin seemed really happy to be part of the crazy family Christmas activities, decorating the tree, finding his personal ornaments my mother had saved, eating all the special food – cookies, fudge, turkey dinner and his favorite, pumpkin pie. He and my dad both wore Christmas stocking caps, behaving playfully in our gathering time. I have a cherished photo of the two of them together in those red and white hats. I did not know it would be our last Christmas together, for both my father and Justin. Justin took the train to Seattle to visit some of his friends before flying back to Kansas City and I flew home from Montana the day after Christmas. A special gift from that trip was in my parting photo of me with my Dad looking straight into the camera, his blue eyes clear and alive.

The next day he went into the hospital with his feeding tube blocked because of all the fudge he had sneaked over the holidays.

He never recovered from that hospital stay. What should have been a simple procedure with him coming home the same day, turned into a three-week process ending with him leaving his body on January 21, 2007, after he developed double pneumonia that quickly overcame him and took his life. I was unable to return to Montana in time to be with him at the end, but I was able to have my sister hold the phone up to his ear so I could tell him I loved him and let him know it was "okay" for him to leave. I could hear his raspy breathing and though he was unconscious by that point, knew he heard me and felt my love, as he soon stopped breathing. In that moment, I felt that a part of me departed along with my father's soul, a surreal moment in time as I experienced the very human reality of life and death.

My father's death was the most truly painful death experience I had of losing a loved one up to that time. I had lost my paternal grandfather at seven, being too young to really understand death, and both my grandmothers, who in their mid-to-late 90's, had died of natural life expectancy and therefore I was not surprised when either transitioned. But my father's death unknowingly helped prepare me for the deeper loss to come six years later, on May 30, 2013.

I processed my sadness by sitting silently in the dark for long periods of time after my father's transition, feeling his presence close to me. One morning I awoke from a dream where I had a realization of a message he had sent to help me understand the process of grief. I felt this inner knowing that to feel deeply no matter what the experience, was important, but especially when from a sad or painful event, to not avoid feeling it, as it was necessary to heal. My awareness was that the vibrations of deep sadness and pain from loss and grief, are the same intensity as joy on the opposite side of the spectrum. When we can feel the full spectrum, from one side to the other, we will be able to experience the fullness of life in more profound and empowering ways. It was very clearly revealed to me that we limited ourselves if we resist feeling either side of the vibrational spectrum, or anything in-between. That insight became the beginning of both my healing from my father's death, and also my willingness to feel deeply, even when, and most especially when life was most painful. Thank you, Dad! I have my picture of our last moment together with his eyes looking as if right at me, and I can feel a connection with him through his eyes in that picture. Such a blessing; I treasure it.

After I was ordained, I accepted a position as an associate minister in Mesa, Arizona, while Justin remained in Kansas City with his girlfriend awaiting the birth of their child. I moved to Arizona in September, just three weeks before I became a grandmother for the first time, missing the birth and the opportunity to hold my son's baby girl. Another life regret I cannot get back, but circumstances did not support my being with him at that time. Justin was over the moon with having a child and his love and devotion is what kept him on track more often than not from that point forward. He truly wanted to be a better person for his little girl's sake. She was his miracle!

What I realize in the world of addiction is that the pull back into substance abuse is very powerful and the so-called friends that draw one into it have a tremendous influence on the one who wants a different life, the one who wants to change. How do you avoid or leave behind the only friends you think you have? How can you isolate yourself from them in what appears to be a lonely path? I know in his heart of hearts Justin wanted to be sober, to improve his life circumstances, to be free of his demons and make his daughter proud as she grew up. But the pull into the abyss was so strong. I had to start setting stronger boundaries in my relationship with him during those years; first, to not let it destroy me; and second, to honor myself and my health and wholeness, my mental stability to function. It was hard, as he was so good at getting to me and using guilt to undermine my convictions. I would beat myself up every time I gave in and sent him funds to keep afloat, knowing he most likely lied to me and used the money to buy beer or something even more dangerous. I tried not to think about it, wanting to believe he needed the one person he could count on, and getting caught up in fear of what might happen if I wasn't there for him.

His relationship with his daughter's mother was also volatile. They lived with her parents, on again and off again, when financially things shifted. The father-in-law became a trigger for Justin, too. He was not a fan of Justin in his daughter's life, and was a controlling and abrasive kind of guy, more of a bully from my observation. Having only one child, he was very controlling of her and she was afraid of going against him. Justin, however, was not, so he became a cause of friction and confrontation. Justin was not one who would back down from anything as I have shared, and though not a big man at 5'11", ranging from about 135-145 pounds, he was extraordinarily strong and rarely ever lost a fight at least not one he would admit to. He would not give up no matter how big the pounding, the threat, or the risk. Often, that made me cringe.

About three months before Justin was taken from this world, he shared with me that he did not think he would have a long life; that he did not have long to live. I don't know if he thought his cancer would return or if it was an inner insight that foretold his death. As his mother, it was not comforting to hear him say such a thing. I remember thinking, *That's crazy, of course you will have a long life, you're only 29 years old!* I thought it was part of his struggle to live in the flow of a life that seemed to work against him. He was prone to often call me in the middle of the night, partly because I was in a different time zone from him, but also it was late at night when he needed a voice to remind him he was loved, someone who would listen and not condemn him. It was his lonely time. I often received 3 a.m. calls from him with a crying voice at the other end saying he felt lost, alone, and not seeing the value in life. It saddened me tremendously, and again, I was not feeling confident in my ability to really help him. So I, too, was lost on some level. But I listened and reminded him he was loved and encouraged him to have the strength to change his life, but it would be up to him to take the first step.

In May of 2013, he was on the brink of making a big change. He had made the decision to leave Kansas City and go back to Eureka, Montana, the place where his maternal grandmother lived, along with some cousins and aunts. He had a job waiting for him with a man he had worked with many years before he moved to Kansas City who believed in him and had a standing job offer for whenever he returned. He claimed Justin was a good worker and saw potential he was willing to cultivate. The only pull for Justin was in not wanting to leave his daughter behind, knowing he would be losing a part of his connection with her and concerned he would be prevented from staying involved in her life. He knew his relationship with his daughter's mother was over, but he was very torn over the prospect of leaving his little girl. His life was moving out of control with his indecisiveness by May 30, 2013, the last day of his life, the last day he took a breath in this physical reality of life … the last day I heard his voice.

On that day he had called me for money. I was living in Pasadena, California, where I was then serving as Senior Minister of a Unity Center. He had been laid off from his job, moved out of his father-in-law's house where his 5-year old daughter was living with her mother, and living on a friend's couch working on his exit plan to Montana. He said he was hungry. What was I to do, say, "Sorry, starve?" Though I was frustrated with him, I told him I would send something anyway, and recall our last conversation being one that reflected my angry feelings of frustration. Looking back, it was one of the most regretful moments of my life. We never know when our last precious connection with someone who matters may be. I sent him $35, not much, but hopefully, I thought, enough to get him by until he could get paid from some of the side jobs he had been doing.

I was preparing to leave a week from that day for a minister's convention at sea, leaving from Fort Lauderdale. I called Justin that following week to let him know I would not have cell access while on board the ship, so wanted to check in with him to say goodbye and see how he was doing. I called several times that week and he had not returned any of my calls. I called once again on my way to the airport … no answer, but I left a message asking him to please call me back.

After two flights, and a long day of traveling, I arrived in Fort Lauderdale around 4 p.m. Eastern Time on June 7, 2013. I was waiting for my bag at baggage claim when I received that fateful call from my older son, who had the most grievous job of telling his mother his brother had been found dead. It was the moment my heart stopped, changing my life forever. Even now, in 2020, seven years later, my mind wants to push that memory away and say "NO, that did not happen, that could not have happened, I won't allow it to have happened." I replay the last moments, the last conversations, the years before that were leading up to this unspeakable moment in time, and nothing changes the outcome.

I remember standing there with my phone in my hand looking at it, and then putting it back to my ear listening to Ryan crying and telling me again, *"He's gone mom, they found his body in a river. A fisherman found him, his face had some damage, they are not sure what happened or how he got in the river ... No, they don't know if he drowned for sure."* How can this be, how can this be... "NOoooooooo" is all my mind can process. I still feel that exact moment in time as if it were permanently embedded into my mind and body, and I guess it has been.

As I shared at the beginning of this book, I had gone white as my partner Michael, said, "What's the matter? What happened?" Other colleagues who had been on the same flight were also standing there and reached out to hold me, not knowing what had happened yet, but seeing a need. I was numb and don't recall if I said anything, but tears rolled down my soundlessly stunned face. I began what was to be my way of managing to be human, going through the motions of being alive but not feeling the reality of being alive.

> *"To be fully alive, fully human, and completely awake is to be continually thrown out of the nest. To live fully is to be always in no-man's land, to experience each moment as completely new and fresh. To live is to be willing to die over and over again."*
> - Pema Chodren (Chödrön, 1997, "Awakening From Grief" p. 71)

PART 2

THE JOURNEY
THROUGH GRIEF

CHAPTER 4

LIFE AFTER

DESTINY - *SPIRITUAL STORY BY UNKNOWN*

"During a momentous battle, a Japanese general decided to attack even though his army was greatly outnumbered. He was confident they would win, but his men were filled with doubt. On the way to battle, they stopped at a religious shrine. After praying with the men, the general took out a coin and said, "I shall now toss this coin. If it is heads, we shall win. If tails, we shall lose. Destiny will now reveal itself."

He threw the coin into the air and all watched intently as it landed. It was heads! The soldiers were so overjoyed and filled with confidence that they vigorously attacked the enemy and were victorious. After the battle, a lieutenant remarked to the general, "No one can change destiny."

"Quite right," the general replied as he showed the lieutenant the coin. It had heads on both sides."

As I write this, tears are streaming down my face recalling the impact of receiving the horrendous news about my son. It still affects me as an emotional punch to the gut that is an internal scream with nowhere to go. I want just one more moment, just one more call to hear his voice, one more time to hug him to me, to feel him in my arms, my little baby boy born just in time for Christmas. I have my last picture of him with me, sitting beside me, speaking to me as I write. And as with the last picture of my father with his eyes looking straight into the camera and into my eyes today, Justin is looking straight into the camera and into my eyes today as if we were looking at each other in person – such a blessed gift! I feel his presence and his soul wanting his story to be told, for his death to make a difference somehow through what I write; through what I can share about grief, the impact of grief, the value of processing grief, and knowing it is possible to live a life after the trauma of grief with meaning and purpose.

While I am still and allow myself to connect with the voice of Spirit, I wonder if his death was a soul agreement for me to dive deep into grief so I can be a teacher of how it serves us? Was his death meant to serve a purpose in how I serve and live my life? Is that why I feel so compelled to share my grief journey as a way to make a difference in the world? In the lives of others who are still struggling with the impact of grief, is it the pain from loss and the insurmountable challenges that grief brings into our life experience?

I feel it somehow is, that Justin came into my life through me to offer a way to teach grief. This includes how it not only offers us a gift, but also the path to know the depth of who we are in a way that enhances who we are; that we are more because we have grieved. In that moment of reflection, I could relate to this quote by Christian author Vance Havner, "*God uses broken things. It takes broken soil to produce a crop, broken clouds to give rain, broken grain to give bread, broken bread to give strength.*" My grief, the seemingly now can be even more, if I allow myself to be used as a result of this pain.

We have so much to learn about what grief offers. Perhaps there is a destiny offered to each of us through our ability to mourn well and embrace all that grief can bring into our life experience. I believe we all have "heads" on both sides of the coin that asks of us – will we believe it is our destiny to win? And by winning, to move courageously into life full throttle without fear or allowing anything, even pain and loss, to hold us back? Perhaps grief is our coin ... our challenge?

As I moved through my days and nights the first few months, I did what I had to in order to get by. I did what I had to, to honor Justin, his life and that he mattered. I did only what I had to do, and perhaps more than I should have done, like going back to serving my ministry after only three weeks. In hindsight, I would have taken more time to not do. I travelled to Seattle to hold a family memorial with my precious boy's ashes a month after his death. We held it at my nephew's waterfront home on the Agate Pass where the Puget Sound flows between the mainland peninsula and Bainbridge Island. Right on the beach, it was the perfect place to remember Justin as a happy, adventurous man who lived life on the edge and would have loved where we celebrated him. I officiated his memorial because I had to as part of my personal healing. To allow all that Justin was and always will be in my heart, to live through me in that moment of honoring his life with those who he mattered to.

We laughed, we cried, we held each other and we sat around sharing Justin stories, getting to know him a little better through each other's memories. Like the one my nephew shared about when he and Ryan had convinced Justin to stuff a little Hot Wheels car tire up his nose. It got stuck and they were afraid to broken part of myself, could give way to a resilient and empowered part of who I have always been, but tell me. Weeks later after he kept getting throat infections and an ear infection that would not heal, the doctor said we had no choice but to have Justin's adenoids and tonsils taken out and an ear tube put in place. After the surgery the doctor came out and showed us the little Hot Wheels tire he had found embedded in his nose that had been causing all the infection. Ryan and his cousin had never fessed up to being the ones to cause that little situation all those years ago, until then, at Justin's memorial service. It was the answer to the question I had asked Justin for years, "Why did you put that teeny tire up your nose, honey?" He would never say – though he was only three years old at the time it happened. It was nice to have some lighter things to focus on that day. That is how a memorial can serve us as we begin our healing process. It can provide the gift of laughter and connection to others in our mutual love for someone we dearly miss. And I forgave those two rascals for never telling me about the hot-wheel shenanigans!

Another gift shared at his memorial was the special music I played of recordings from two of the most amazing singer/songwriters of the New Thought music genre I have the privilege to know and call friends. They had each sent me songs to support me in my healing after hearing about my loss. One a special song written especially about Justin called "Always Love" by Harold Payne – who I will forever be grateful for taking the time to know who Justin was and write about him in a way that reflected his life and loves through song. The other song is called "Precious Child" by Karen Taylor Good from her album *Forever In My Heart*. Karen sent me the download to support me in my healing, and tears still flow down my face every time I listen to this beautiful song about the precious gift a child will always be in a mother's heart. Thank you, Karen and Harold, for sharing your gifts with my family and me in remembrance of my sweet boy.

**Song lyrics to offer comfort and love to those grieving a child – you can download the song for free from this link provided by Karen Taylor Good:
http://www.grievingparent.com/resources/audiovideo
precious-child-by-karen-taylor-good/

PRECIOUS CHILD

By Karen Taylor Good

In my dreams, you are alive and well
Precious child, precious child
In my mind, I see you clear as a bell
Precious child, precious child
In my soul, there is a hole
That can never be filled
But in my heart, there is hope
'Cause you are with me still

In my heart, you live on
Always there, never gone
Precious child, you left too soon
Though it may be true that we're apart
You will live forever, in my heart

In my plans, I was the first to leave
Precious child, precious child
But in this world, I was left here to grieve
Precious child, my precious child
In my soul, there is a hole

That can never be filled
But in my heart, there is hope
And you are with me still

In my heart, you live on
Always there, never gone
Precious child, you left too soon
Though it may be true that we're
apart You will live forever, in my heart

God knows I want to hold you
See you, touch you
And maybe there's a heaven
And someday I will again
Please know, you are not forgotten
Until then

In my heart, you live on
Always there, never gone
Precious child, you left too soon
Though it may be true that we're apart
You will live forever, in my heart

I had nightmares for months after Justin's death. I was afraid to sleep because when I closed my eyes all I could see was my imagined last moment of his life. Was he afraid? Was he in pain? Did he know what happened? Why had this happened, and who could have caused it? I was soon to learn that Justin had been murdered. He had not fallen into the river accidentally, but had been intentionally thrown into it. The coroner confirmed he had been shot three times, once in the back of the head, once in the chest and once in his left eye, and he would have died within seconds, not knowing what had happened to him. Though grateful he apparently had not suffered, the news he had been shot was a horror show for a mother. But what disturbed my sense of humanity more than anything was in what some human beings had chosen to do to my son's body after taking his life. He had been found wrapped in a heavy chain attached to a cinder block and thrown into the river with hope of his body disappearing forever and never being discovered. I was suddenly grateful that he had been found in only five days, as the thought of never having known what happened to him was a worse reality. I don't know what I would have done if I had to live with never knowing what happened to him, that he would have just disappeared forever, never being heard from again.

I know some people have had to live with that reality. And to them, I honor you in this most horrific circumstance. I hold you in my heart to let your soul know you are not alone in your grief. And to support you in releasing whatever is preventing you from living from a sense of purpose and intention, meaning and gratitude. For only when we can release that pain, can we live again freely. I hold that in my heart for you.

I speak from words of personal experience in knowing that. But it has taken time to embrace the reality of the grief my son's murder set into motion. I have learned to make friends with tears, to let them flow without attempting to hold them back; to accept them as a natural way to release and heal emotional pain and sadness. There is a comfort in letting tears flow; that is why I say, make friends with your tears – especially you men! There is nothing weak about crying, it is a demonstration of strength and comfort in your own skin, that you have the capacity to feel. To be real, authentic, and vulnerable is the strongest form of being human. That is why grief becomes our teacher, and a gift in our human experience. It challenges us to be more than we ever thought we could, and more of our true nature in our greatest expression.

As I took a step into each day after Justin's death I began to see my life as Before and After, for it was in the moment between I changed. I would forever be changed because of that moment at baggage claim in Fort Lauderdale on June 7, 2013. I lived a whole week not knowing my son had been dead that entire time I had been trying to reach him. That shook me, too! I was calling into nothing, for no one was going to answer, his voice would never be spoken into his phone for me to hear again. I kept calling his phone for weeks after learning of his death, just hoping maybe they had been wrong, that maybe he had just lost his charger and finally got reconnected. Eventually his number had been reassigned to someone else so when I called it months down the road because I could not help myself, someone else answered and I had to accept the reality he would not be on the other end of line ever again. The man who answered was gracious in understanding my grief and I assured him I would not call again. That was a moment of moving toward acceptance, a time I was ready to begin accepting, a little bit.

But in the first few weeks of processing the reality of what happened, I thought maybe because he was not visually recognizable after five days in the river with the face damage from a gunshot, maybe they had wrongly identified him? Our minds play some really vivid games when we are in denial of reality or of facts that have been presented. It is part of the grief process; we live in denial for as long as it takes to accept that the reality we want deep in our soul will never come to pass.... We struggle with accepting there is nothing we can do to reset the clock, or time, or reality. What we cling to more than anything is like grasping at sand, it will not come to fruition. So it changes us at our core. Just like that, what we lost will never be again, whether it is a loved one, or property, or a relationship, or a job. It is something we can no longer have, experience or live with, we can never be the person we were in the moment before loss happened and triggered grief to rise up within us.

So in my "After days," I began to sit with my grief, my pain, my loss, my emotions, my thoughts and become an observer of them. I have learned from my study of the spiritual teachings of Buddhism that attachment is the root of all suffering, and observation without attachment allows us to see what we may not have noticed before. Before, we were in the drama of our emotions or consumed with the feelings that take over, especially in the grief experience. So I began to observe what has happening within me. And asking a lot of questions: What am I to learn from this experience? What am I resisting around this experience? What do I need to forgive from this experience? What do I need to do to heal and support myself from this experience? What is the gift in this experience? I went through a process of redirecting emotions from what we can't have or make happen or resisting the things that cause our suffering, to what can I do or learn or realize to support me in this now moment of reality.

Slowly, I began to realize I was feeling gratitude! I know, "WHAT?" How could that be? But a very deep sense of gratitude was very present in my moments. As I asked what that was, the answer came to me: because Justin chose to come into this lifetime through me. Tears well up again remembering that moment. Justin was a gift for my soul-learning, my soul-evolution, my soul-growth. I was grateful, too, for all the love and compassion that poured out to me as I navigated this unasked-for life experience. People I never knew cared called or sent me cards, or asked if I needed a ride, or needed someone to sit with me. My heart was overwhelmed with the kindness that entered my world. I was grateful for my spiritual foundation that gave me a place to ground myself, without which I may have just stayed in bed for months. Many asked me how could I possibly get out of bed, get dressed, and show up for anything, let alone doing my Sunday messages and conducting services. I think it was because I thought I had to, I had to persevere no matter what *(that part of me that was in Justin, and maybe he received from me?).* And that maybe I was holding back for fear I would completely collapse if I let go and stopped doing. I recognize *"Doing is something we human beings can do really well when we are avoiding doing nothing instead."*

I do realize the initial months of numbness were really a divinely imbedded gift of life to help us absorb the impact of shock. They provided a natural shock absorber to not have to take on the full impact of a traumatic life experience. If we had to process it all at once it could surely be more than we could take on, and our hearts may stop. So as the numbness gradually wears off, the impact of the pain can seem to increase. We are beginning to experience the fullness of the loss and all it means for a changed reality. We may again go into a denial stage, which is why we are told from a psychological perspective that the process of grief is like two steps forward, one step back and all over the map. We may become angrier because accepting something we don't want to accept feels unfair or unjust or cruel. Why should I have to deal with this when I never wanted it? Why, why?

I also realized from my already established spiritual belief system that self-care during a time of healing from pain and loss is vitally important. I considered what I needed to support my body, mind, and soul in my experience of intense grief. I chose to eat simple yet healthy meals. Things I could easily prepare but also easily digest with my unsettled stomach. Whole fresh food, no processed or junk food – only what would provide the nourishment my body needed to process the extra energy it takes to heal pain. I did include a bit of good dark chocolate, as I think it must surely contain healing properties we need!

I began intense walking as a process to release my anger and frustration and to allow healing to begin. Though I had already been a walker as a form of meditation before Justin's death, it was natural for me to simply increase my walking but through a more intentional process. To actively move my body helped to process the thoughts that were constantly running through my mind. To shift to more proactive thinking and thoughts that supported me rather than dragging me into the pain my heart had become drunk on when living in it.

I also was blessed to have access to a pool in the yard of my little rented guesthouse, so swimming became a much needed source of healing for me. I could float in the pool and let my tears mingle with the water as it gently held me up and cradled me like a soothing hug wrapped around my whole body. I spent a lot of time in that pool, another thing I became extraordinarily grateful for. I had found myself in the perfect place to heal the magnitude of such a horrendous loss. I also had a hot tub for my use connected to the lovely pool, so my evenings became a warm healing time bathed in the jetted water, relaxing my body and mind to allow for the possibility of sleep. I took naps when I could, to sleep as an escape from the activity of my thoughts in my awake state. I bathed my heart in soothing music, often songs that allowed cleansing tears to flow. I listened to what my body told me it needed and honored that voice.

"Sometimes the purpose of a day is to merely feel our sadness, knowing that as we do, we allow whole layers of grief, like old skin cells, to drop off us."

~ Marianne Williamson (2004). "Everyday Grace: Having Hope, Finding Forgiveness, and Making Miracles", Penguin

I think my process of listening, feeling, moving, and caring was doing what Marianne suggested, allowing layers of grief, *"like old skin cells to drop off us.* I was dropping off the old cells of pain I had been using up to allow for new and healed cells of acceptance to replace them.

In my observation I began to draw from my spiritual teachings of forgiveness. One never knows how they will be able to truly forgive until confronted with something that seems unforgivable. I have had a lifetime of practice from an abusive husband and other human relationship challenges, but nothing tested my practice more than the murder of my son. In practice, forgiveness is something we do for ourselves, not to let anyone or anything off the hook, or out of accountability or responsibility. If we understand the concept of universal spirituality or metaphysics that everything is energy, including our thoughts, feelings, emotions, and physical manifestations, then we can accept that forgiveness is releasing the energy of anger, fear, resentment, or judgment of or toward others to free us of the bondage that intense energy imprisons us in. To not forgive is like what someone once said, *"Unforgiveness is like swallowing poison and expecting the other person to die."* We slowly kill ourselves with the energy of unforgiveness.

So I recognized the importance of intentionally practicing forgiveness in order to heal and move forward in healthier and more empowering ways. I do not pretend to say it was easy … it was one of the most challenging spiritual exercises of my life. By this point, the detectives on the case had begun to discover new information and that opened the door to a new set of emotional triggers every time they shared with me something they had discovered. It felt like I was starting over with every call, but I also knew it was important for me to stay committed to the philosophy I teach others, or how could I stand in integrity?

I began with forgiving my ex-husband all over again for his part in Justin's anger and rage in life and his self-destructive path that I believed led him to where he was at the end of his life. I speculated that Justin may have otherwise been in a better place if things had been different with his relationship with his father. Renewed anger and emotional triggers were set off throughout the first few months after Justin's death from the need to communicate with his father after so many years. We had divorced in 1987, so 2013 was a very long time to have healed from that time in my life and to have moved on. However, his father, who I will not name, stepped in to take over the whole process of how Justin's body was handled, where and when it was cremated, how the ashes were transported from Kansas City to Seattle, and where and when the memorial would happen, and where his ashes would be placed for remembrance. He insisted on paying for everything. I accepted that, as I believed it was something he needed to do to heal from his rejection of Justin so many years before. At first, I was invited and then uninvited to attend the memorial he planned when he decided he wasn't comfortable with me participating. I was also not invited to be part of placing Justin's ashes where he is now memorialized next to his paternal grandfather who transitioned the same year a few months before Justin. Months later, and long after the fact, I was called and asked how much was I willing to reimburse him for all he had spent? Without ever having had a say in any of the decisions, and his having overspent in many areas that could have had a different financial choice made, he had put himself in a bind and thought I could just split it with him … so let's just say I did not handle that conversation well. Forgiveness became necessary repeatedly over the course of time processing Justin's death. What is it said about achieving success? Practice, practice, practice? Well forgiveness is something we get to practice for a lifetime.

I began my forgiveness practice with my son's father and the unnamed beings responsible for Justin's death, as they had not yet been apprehended at that point and I had no names to focus forgiveness on. Even without knowing the names, I knew it was spiritually important to forgive if I were to heal my heart and mind, so I made a choice to forgive all those involved in any way in Justin's death. I used the affirmation *"I release, forgive, and let go anyone or anything that no longer supports my highest and best interest in manifesting unconditional love, prosperity, peace, and wholeness."* I used that to begin, to live in that intention each day. My intention was to see the energy connection to whomever I felt unforgiveness, anger or negativity toward, breaking up, dissolving and releasing me from the bondage it had held over me. I envisioned the release and felt the freedom experienced from the process, then gave thanks for it as a gift in my healing.

My greatest gifts in this grief journey have been acceptance, forgiveness, and gratitude. It is not something we sit around and say to ourselves, "Hmmm, I think this horrific experience that ripped my heart out and shredded my very existence offers me the most amazing gifts – oh yes, they are acceptance, forgiveness and gratitude of course – NOT!" It was a process where I could look and see what was happening in the midst of unraveling my grief, to see it for what it was, so I could begin to embrace the gifts revealed and move forward, discovering a new sense of meaning and purpose in my life. That was not obvious at the beginning, but it is what I realized during the journey.

I compare the healing process of grief that brought me into the awareness of the gifts within the broken parts of my heart to something I discovered more recently, with the Japanese pottery art form known as *Kintsugi*, meaning "golden joinery." *Kintsugi* is the process in which breaks and repairs in pottery are treated as part of the object's history rather than broken and useless. Artisans trained in *Kintsugi* carefully mend broken ceramics using a lacquer resin that has been mixed with powdered gold, silver, or platinum. The repairs are visible yet somehow beautiful with precious metals shining boldly from the cracks as they hold the broken pieces together. The broken articles become enhanced and even more valuable because of the cracks, rather than something to be discarded and lost. They continue to hold value and the cracks serve as a reminder of the life and history of their existence. Truly, they have gifts hidden within the breaks, which are caused from living.

In my grief journey, I have found many golden moments that have added value and become cherished gifts. The "golden resin," I can now say, has helped to mend my broken heart and rejoin the shattered pieces I once felt would never function with any level of vitality again. The little moments that gratitude, acceptance, and forgiveness provide are – the spiritual lacquer components that make up the healing union that is our wholeness, offering a reminder of the profound experience our willingness to unravel grief offers. It is transformational at its roots and empowering at its core.

Kintsugi is a reminder that love is the "golden joinery" of life, as well. And that grief is our deepest reminder and most profound teacher of the value of loving we can ever experience. I love the analogy of something that is taught as a valuable way of preserving what we love and realizing there is a way to maintain it as part of our life even though it may have been broken and is no longer manifesting in its original form. I correlate this concept in a quote by author Jamie Anderson, *"Grief, I've learned, is really just love. It's all the love you want to give but cannot. All of that unspent love gathers up in the corners of your eyes, the lump in your throat, and in that hollow part of your chest. Grief is just love with no place to go."* By choosing to use the spiritual gifts of acceptance, forgiveness, and gratitude as tools, we can find a place to share our love as we intentionally unravel and ultimately embrace grief as a transformational process.

I remember the first Christmas after Justin's death, six months from the time his life was taken; it has a special memory for me now. A couple of gifts showed up for me around December 14, what would have been his thirtieth birthday. Remember, I shared earlier how Justin would often call me in the middle of the night to talk and cry and to be heard and feel accepted. After he died my phone starting lighting up around 3 a.m., the time he frequently called me, but there was no call, just a light came on. I spoke with a psychic medium who said that often departed souls will reach out to connect via electronics because, yes, it is energy and the easiest way to connect vibrationally. Makes sense, so he suggested it was Justin checking in to let me know he was near and still reaching out to know I was not alone. It was a comfort for me to think that may be true, so I believe it was him. Suddenly after December 14, 2013, the 3 a.m. phone-lighting-up incidents stopped and has never occurred again … proof enough for me it was his way of saying, "I'm around, I'm okay, and now I am ready to move on."

On December 14 that year, on his thirtieth birthday, it was also the night the local neighborhood had its annual Christmas Tree Lighting Ceremony on Christmas Tree Lane – a one mile stretch of road that has these beautiful 100-year-old Italian pine trees that were probably over 50 feet high on both sides of the street reaching across and touching their branches in the middle forming an arch. Each year, they are strung with hundreds of Christmas lights. When they were lit, they created a magical experience of driving up a fairyland entrance that made the child within jump with delight. The mayor and city dignitaries, along with the neighbors, all gather at the top of the street where the local high school marching band stands ready to play, many dressed in Christmas costumes. A parade is started after a few appropriate speeches and words of thanks to all the hundreds of volunteers it took to string the lights, with everyone joining behind the marching band playing Christmas songs as the lights come to life. It was an amazing experience and in my mind all in celebration of Justin's thirtieth birthday, marking the first Christmas without him a special healing moment for me. Justin loved Christmas, being born just in time for it after all, and would have loved that special lighting of the trees on his birthday that year. Tears of love and joy added to the parade, though I am sure no one else really noticed, as it was dark except for the beautiful lights.

I also began what has now become a ritual for me each Christmas. I bought a metal Christmas ornament of a red stocking and the year 2013 engraved on it with a round space to insert a picture. I inserted one of my favorite school pictures of Justin from first grade, before he became so jaded in life and his sweet innocence had yet to be diminished, and hung it on my tree that year. I also lit a special candle each night from his birthday to Christmas morning, both of which I continue to do each year in remembrance of him, but also to feel his presence as a part of my Christmas experience every year. I love to look at that specially placed ornament and see his smiling little face beaming at me as if he never grew up and is always with me. And he is. Somehow I feel his presence stronger now than I ever did when he was in the density of his physical body. He is always with me. All I have to do is close my eyes and see him, as I knew him, and feel him with me. I knew then, in that moment in 2014, that I was on my way back.

CHAPTER 5

MOVING FORWARD

"And suddenly you know: It's time to start something new and trust the magic of beginnings."
~ Meister Eckhart

Now, as I have moved forward in this continuous process of healing, transforming, and living with grief, I am coming into the greater purpose of what my grief journey is about. The "why"' in using grief as a spiritual teacher offers me the chance to express what I have experienced, learned, and healed from with others. It has taken all these years to get clarity but there has been a subtle inner calling, a nudge to pay attention to what I am to do with this experience from my life. As I was feeling restless and my creative energy cut off and frustrated and unfulfilled, I decided it was time to begin listening and observing to what that was about. To again, use what I have been learning and teaching since 1995. Remember, the practice never stops. What came up for me was to shift the form of ministry I was engaged in and move in another direction. I had been co-ministering with my husband for about four-and-a-half years in Cincinnati, in the Southwest Region of Ohio, and the unrest I felt was also showing up in our ministry; I knew I was being called to change on many levels. A part of me felt as if I would dissolve inside if I did not make some changes. For years, I also had been called to write this book to share how unraveling grief to embrace life and live a more meaningful life as a result of grief was possible after tragedy, pain, and loss. I had just ignored the urges, not feeling I was ready.

As I remained open to what might support me in moving in a new direction, I stumbled across the coaching designation of grief. Grief coaching was a certification, who knew? That was what I had been searching for, the next step in my education and training to allow me to step into a new form of ministry and supporting others in healing painful life experiences. I signed up for the online course and began the educational process right away, knowing in my heart it was what I was meant to do. It was the beginning of something I was setting into motion, not even knowing what it might be opening up within me to do next. And synchronistically, as the wisdom within frequently inspires us in the right timing for the most empowering results, when Michael and I stepped down from our ministry earlier than anticipated in May 2019, mid-course training, I had already set into motion the first piece of my new life. It was as George Eliot said in her writing, *Middlemarch: A Study of Provincial Life,* "She was no longer wrestling with the grief, but could sit down with it as a lasting companion and make it a sharer in her thoughts".

The previous fall, I had begun exploring other creative modalities with acrylic painting, and I believe that activated the creative process within me to churn things up and get my attention again. Grief has a way of shutting down our creative expression, something our souls need as much as air to breathe. I had not realized how much of myself had been locked away for so long. It was now calling to me to set free what I had long forgotten. I began having some fun with colors and paints, and even was inspired to create a special painting for each of my four sisters and my mother as gifts that Christmas. Openly sharing my creativity was a new level of vulnerability. I intentionally chose to put myself out there, but with the purpose of having fun with it and not worrying what anyone thought of my talent – or at least not as much as I normally would have.

In the midst of my grief coaching training, it became more clear it was time to step down from serving a spiritual community. It was not the timing I had imagined for myself, but the energy I felt within was telling me that is was. The current circumstances had become more hostile and mentally and emotionally exhausting. I felt on a cellular level if I did not actively cause change in my environment, I would end up seriously ill. So I had to ask myself, "Do I have the courage to let go?" Of course there was a universal push presented in the outer reality to make it feel like stepping off the edge of a cliff, and created a whole lot of painful emotional energy to be processed as a result. But I knew that no matter how overwhelmingly challenging it felt, I was equipped to take it on, and it was something my husband and I chose to do together. To move into what was next for us at the same time, but realizing most likely in different forms of "next." We consciously made this decision as we searched our souls for guidance and considered, individually: did we have the courage to let go of what was impacting our ability to thrive mentally, emotionally, and spiritually? The call of freedom and release became greater than holding onto what was and living in the pain of the experience. So the answer was a unanimous "yes."

It is interesting how one can feel hurt and grateful at the same time. Another form of grief had stepped into my life, but the new sense of freedom that resulted was enormous! By now I am better at recognizing what grief is and how it serves a purpose if we are willing to unravel it one step at a time and process it; to explore what it may be offering and then have the courage to accept whatever it is and use it to enhance a new life reality. We knew in the process we are creating a new life experience by leaving behind something in a form that was either no longer an option or was no longer serving my potential to create and thrive.

Something else I now know about grief is that none of us living on this planet now or from the beginning of time can ever escape the experience of grief. It is part of the human experience, so to attempt to avoid it only deepens our pain. It serves a purpose, if we are willing to embrace it. Unresolved grief impacts us in so many ways. Unresolved grief is what we carry with us into every experience in life if we have not intentionally processed it every time it shows up. It is the little things we don't always notice that can sabotage us later by collectively being added to the next painful loss in life, especially a big one like my son's murder, if we have not processed grief along the way. It is no wonder that for many, the experience of grief immobilizes them and destroys their quality of life.

I now know I will be impacted by Justin's death for the rest of my life. Little things can trigger the emotional feelings all over again, but usually with less intensity than the initial impact. I did have another big grief jolt when eighteen months after my son's murder, two young men were arrested for his death. That in itself set off an internal emotional scream. But it was also surprisingly revealed there were others who were close to him who were responsible and contributed to his murder. They were initially arrested and released, but have yet to be prosecuted because the evidence that would have linked them to the crime had been destroyed. The legal system will not prosecute a case without physical evidence, as it cannot convict on hearsay. There is verbal evidence from one of the defendants arrested who gave information that provided more details of who was involved and what had transpired, but there is nothing to back up his version of the facts, so it is still an open case at this point. I cannot say anything more about it as it is an ongoing investigation, but it is an open wound for me that may never be closed. When I began to hear more details about what happened to my son, and the last moments of his life, and even more the reason for his intentional death, my heart was sickened.

One clear thing I have had to tell myself over and over again is that I can never put myself into the mind of someone who has chosen to take another's life or participate in something legally, morally, or spiritually wrong. So I will not let myself go crazy trying to understand the "why." There is no why in a case like this. People do things as human beings from fear, a survival need, a place of needing to control, which is fear based, a lack of compassion or concern for life – meaning something is out of balance within them, or not being aware of the Divine Nature living within them – that would not make those choices. People make choices based on our human conditions, human experiences, and human understandings, which is solely based on the world outside of ourselves. When we are in sync with our Divine Nature, aware and choosing to go within to seek guidance and perspective and not react to life, we will NEVER choose to take a life unless it is to save ourselves or another's in an act of self-defense. Nor would we break a law or act from a mean-spirited heart or share gossip without considering the truth or intentionally hurt others, for it would be impossible for us to choose such actions. I know that those who chose to kill my son or knowingly participated in his murder did not take actions from a place of awareness or guidance from their Divine Nature. It was their human and spiritually immature thinking that led them into inappropriate actions. That is how I can forgive them. Yet I am still triggered by my human emotions and my feelings when something outside of me happens that is painful, our human nature is vulnerable to those triggers.

The judicial process of charging and convicting those accused of a crime is not like TV. It is slow and tedious and full of setbacks and disappointments that make no sense to those of us outside the system. Eventually the two arrested with the physical responsibility of my son's murder made plea bargains with the prosecutor after nearly two years waiting in jail. So no trial was held; perhaps that was a blessing. The defendant who actually fired the gun that took Justin's life was sentenced to twenty-two years with fifteen years minimum before being eligible for parole. The other defendant was given fourteen years with no minimum in exchange for testimony to assist in the case to prosecute the others involved. Nothing has come from that as of late Summer, 2020. That individual was up for parole in April of 2018, a shock to me at the time. He was not released then, but did come up for parole again in April 2020. I was preparing to attend that hearing, but because of the Covid-19 stay-at-home orders, I was unable to attend. I therefore submitted a written and audio-recorded statement to be shared when he went before the Parole Board Hearing. Trusting he would not be considered ready to be released at this time, I was again shocked at their decision to set his release date for December 2023, with the rest of his sentence to be served on probation. Something I am processing at the same time realizing I have no control over their decision and must come to accept it for what it is.

It was explained to me that since the defendant had no minimum years to serve before being eligible for parole, it was normal for it to come up right away. And in the State of Missouri, where the crime took place and the defendants are serving prison time, all prisoners are released on parole before serving a full sentence so they will be supervised for the last years of their sentence to assist them in adjusting back into society. This is done to monitor them during that time; otherwise they would not be monitored or provided assistance. They would be left on their own and there is a higher percentage of repeat offending without parole and monitoring. So it is best for all concerned when it is explained that way.

When I received the notice for the first parole hearing, everything came up fresh for me again. I had to relive moments I wanted to bury and process my emotions anew. I also realized that it was important for me to attend the hearing to exercise my voice since I didn't have that chance because there was no trial. I have been blessed to be assigned a victim advocate. Even though I do not like the word "victim," the advocate stays in touch with me, keeps me informed of what is happening, explains what is happening or why, and was there for me when I attended the first hearing in 2018.

The hearings are held in the state's capital city of Jefferson City at the judicial building while the defendant stays at the prison, but is on camera for everyone in the hearing room to see and hear. That provided the opportunity for me to both see and hear him, but he could only hear me, not see me, as I was seated outside the camera's range. That makes the whole process safer and less vulnerable for anyone in the position I was then.

In the hearing, I was allowed to make a statement. I was encouraged to write what I wanted to say beforehand to prevent the emotions of the moment from interfering with what I especially wanted to say, so I came prepared with my written statement to read out loud. The defendant was respectful and seemed to acknowledge what I said. He had only been nineteen years old when arrested, so at twenty-three was still very young. His mother was sitting next to him in support. Along with my statement, I also read a statement from Justin's brother, Ryan, who had some very strong things he wanted shared as he could not travel to Missouri to be there in person. The words I shared at the beginning of this book came from the portion of my statement that described my emotions and feelings that the actions of those responsible triggered within me. I wanted that young man to hear the significant impact his actions had made on not only my life, but on everyone connected to the whole horrendous outcome, triggered in part by his choices: Justin's life, my life, Justin's brother's life, his daughter, all my family, his family, his friends and so many others.

What happened in that hearing after my sharing is what really shook me in a way I was unprepared to experience. As the head parole officer proceeded to ask the defendant very specific questions about his role in the crime for which he was convicted and for which he was now in prison, and to walk them through the whole event, I was breathless. I had not heard the level of details shared prior to that day and it revealed some things that both put more of the pieces together, but also were very hard to hear spoken out loud. I realize it served to assist me in having more closure, if that is even possible, and was necessary for a deeper level of healing, but still painful to listen to on any level.

The details of how Justin was killed and what happened afterward, how they got paid to kill him, and how they decided to dispose of his body after the fact – with guidance from the one who paid them and one of the individuals still free from being accountable for their actions – took me to a place outside my body where I was observing what was happening in the room. It was more like I was watching a movie about someone else's life, except it was mine, and the ending of my son's life. I was stunned when I realized the level of planning and devious action that had come into play in carrying out my son's murder. To take his life from him because someone else did not want him around, made me speechless; it was so heart-wrenching. This was my little boy they were talking about.

The victim advocate continues to stay in touch with me to keep me informed of anything that comes up regarding my son's case or information that may be relevant for me to be aware of. One is that there is a National Crime Victim's Rights Awareness Week every year around the third week in April. Most states have some form of events or programs for the public to create more awareness of the support and resources available to those who have been victimized in any way. I became aware of the NCVRW events in Missouri when my advocate contacted me in March of 2019 to ask if they could share a portion of my statement from the parole hearing the previous year as part of their program in 2019. She said many people find it difficult to voice their feelings around what happened to them and my words would be helpful in giving them a way to describe their feelings. I was honored to be asked and of course granted them permission to share my words – the portion I shared in the Introduction of this book.

This relationship with the advocacy support within the Missouri State Department of Justice has developed to my being invited to be their keynote speaker for both the candlelight vigil event at the beginning of the week of events and the main event in the capitol rotunda midweek for NCVRW in April 2020. This was to have occurred as I was in the editing process of this book, so it would have happened by the time this book is published. However, just as I was not able to attend the April 20 parole hearing, the live events for the NCVRW week in 2020 were cancelled, and I am intentionally trusting I will be invited back to speak at their 2021 events. I had been thrilled to be the voice for those who may not have found a way to process their grief, anger, or unforgiveness. My intention is still to invite anyone who may be listening at any event I speak at, or who is reading this book, to know that what has happened to you matters. That there is a way to heal as we take courageous steps forward to both learn to live with the results of our experiences, but also to transform and reinvent our lives to use what has happened to enhance who we are – to not be labeled as victims, but survivors of life and empowered, knowing everyone can manage anything life tosses at them with strength, grace, and perseverance.

I mentioned before my dislike of the word "victim." Technically, it is defined in the dictionary as anyone *"harmed, injured, or killed as a result of a crime, accident, or other event or action." Or in another description, "A person who has suffered physical or emotional harm, property damage, or economic loss as a result of a crime."* It also can include a relative or dependent of the "victim," as I am categorized because my son was a victim of a crime. But often the word *victim* insinuates weakness or someone who cannot stand up for themselves or is incapable of helping themselves. I am not a fan of that implication. I do not see myself as victimized, weak, incapable, or helpless. I believe when we believe that about ourselves we remain stuck in a place that prevents us from moving forward in healthy and empowered ways.

Because people react to adversity in different ways, we can be susceptible to developing a victim consciousness, a victim way of thinking, if we are not paying attention to our thoughts, words, and actions. I realize I could easily have developed a victim state of mind from the years of domestic abuse and trauma I experienced even before my son was murdered. Instead I believe I have been able to focus on seeking a positive outcome or guidance to support me overcoming whatever negative circumstances I have experienced. I automatically seek resources to support my needs, how to manage what is happening or whatever will assist me in the moment. Behavior that might be called "survivor mentality," or survivor consciousness. But I have developed it by building a spiritual foundation in my life. I have built up the resilience factors present before the trauma happens. In the moment of trauma, we then naturally reveal other abilities to serve us in ways that assist us in managing the circumstances because of that foundation being in place beforehand. That would be our goal in dealing with grief. To have a survivor consciousness in life will always serve us in profound ways no matter the situation in which we find ourselves.

It is also important to notice if you may be living in a victim consciousness so you can intentionally choose to take action to change or shift your thinking and your behavior. To know whether you are developing a "victim consciousness," notice if you are exhibiting any of the following behaviors:

- You feel powerless, unable to solve a problem or cope effectively with it.

- You tend to see your problems as catastrophic.

- You tend to think others are purposefully trying to hurt you.

- You believe you alone are targeted for mistreatment.

- You hold tightly to thoughts and feelings related to being a victim.

If you notice any of those behaviors or thought processes, don't beat yourself up. Take a breath and consider a different thought or action you could take that would produce a more positive result or more positive response. Shift to courageous action and thinking, even if scared, overwhelmed, or emotionally distraught. Instead of focusing on "what is happening to me," choose to focus on what "can I do to empower me" in this moment. Moments of feeling any of those things do not make you a victim, but a person in the midst of pain. The important thing to be aware of is that lingering in those thoughts, feelings, or behaviors is what will move you in the direction of developing the personality trait of victim consciousness, or technically known as victim mentality, and make it more challenging to choose a survivor action. Self-care, allowing yourself to feel all your pain and process it, is also survivor consciousness or behavior.

So when I was in the parole hearing room listening to the additional horror reality of what happened to my son, I felt the initial shock ripple through me and acknowledged it for what it was. Being provided the missing information that filled in the gaps of knowing what happened in the last moments of my son's life was important knowledge. And I can honestly say I am grateful to know more of the truth…see how gratitude sneaks into the most unlikely places? As hard as it was to hear the information I was listening to, I was grateful to know the truth, finally to have put the missing pieces in place in my mind. It is so important in our process of health and wholeness to find gratitude where we can… that is survivor thinking, too. It is a vital energy that lifts us up to experiencing the vibration of life that aligns us with our source, that which we call God. What I have learned about grief is you cannot process, heal, and transform the energy from pain and loss without gratitude as a result. It is a natural part of who we are that is suppressed in unresolved grief. And we cannot get to gratitude in victim thinking, as that keeps us stuck in all the destructive aspects of grief.

One can say unresolved grief is at the core of much of our life sickness and disease. Unresolved grief, like unforgiveness, keeps us stuck in negative and lower vibrational energy and prevents our alignment with our natural state of vibrational wholeness. Our bodies cannot respond to support us when emotionally we are shut down in negativity and pain. I have witnessed so many times those who are reeling from the pain of the death of a loved one, especially of a child, and have been unable to process their feelings, emotions, or come to any terms of acceptance in their child's death. I can put myself in their place and understand the pain, but I can also lovingly ask, "Do you think your loved one would want you to choose to stop living because of what happened to them? What about the cherished memories you have in your heart and mind? Would you be willing to give them up to have the pain of your loss go away?" I have never had anyone say they would trade their memories. Living in the pain prevents the possibility of living in the world. At some point, we must choose what is most important. To live in the pain so intensely we cannot function for the rest of our lives, potentially losing everything that is left? To lose relationships, a job, our home when we cannot pay our bills or ultimately become homeless? It happens, it is tragic. One tragedy triggers another tragedy and there is no life potential left to continue the creative process we are all designed to live in, as and through. Or do you choose life? To choose to allow the activity of Godness within us that can lead us forward to heal, transform, and manifest a life that supports thriving and abundance.

Those are some of the compelling reasons I am called to support anyone impacted by grief. I know the traps, pitfalls and stuck realities we can find ourselves in the midst of grief. I also know there is a way through it, to discover the gift that will enhance who we are, leading us to live more productive meaningful lives – even because of what has happened in our lives. "We must embrace pain and burn it as fuel for our journey," says *Kenji Miyazawa,* a Japanese novelist. And therefore, there is a way forward.

CHAPTER 6

WHAT IS GRIEF?

"Sad is good. Let sadness be a connector for you with humanity. Let sadness connect you with life. Life has sadness and life has joy … life has hard times and life has beautiful times. It's a complete picture, and you can't live a human life without all those aspects being a part of it. It is some kind of myth that you could avoid all the painful parts and just have the pleasant parts. That's definitely never going to happen. Everybody tries and it never happens. They keep trying anyway. So the fact that it hurts and you feel sad, think of that as actually good. Think of that as growth, that sometimes that is what growth feels like."
~ Pema Chodron

So what is grief? What does it really mean? I like what Wikipedia has to say about what grief is, as it gets into the depth of grief: *"a multifaceted response to loss, particularly to the loss of someone or something that has died, to which a bond or affection was formed. Although conventionally focused on the emotional response to loss, it also has physical, cognitive, behavioral, social, cultural, spiritual, and philosophical dimensions."*

Wow, that means we can be impacted by grief from the possibility of so many variables in life, that we could be affected by something in impactful ways more often than we realize. Where are we educated about the significant impact of grief in our lives? Where do we include it as important in learning about how to navigate life? Unfortunately, as people in the world, we are not educated about or include grief as important in navigating life. We are left to learn by trial and error, or observation, and hope for the best for the most part. Which does not work well in our favor – have you noticed?

I have become aware that death, especially, is an event our society encourages us to avoid, cheat, hide, delay, and deny, even though it pervades our daily lives with every experience of loss we encounter. Consequently, we are further conditioned to limit the duration, intensity, and open expressions of our grief. So it does explain why we are so prone to not seek support or choose to process grief as it shows up, but to carry it along with us unresolved until it finally implodes with the significant tragedies of our lives. Many times, it leaves us impaled with the magnitude of the pain that has accumulated along the way so that we are left with no real understanding of the grief that has taken up residence in our *"physical, cognitive, behavioral, social, cultural, spiritual, and philosophical dimensions."*

I recently listened to an interview between Howard Stern and Anderson Cooper; the conversation evolved into discussing the pain from loss after each experiencing a parents death. They were very open about the experience of grief and how it touched their lives and how it impacted and changed them as a result. What got my attention was when they both agreed how we human beings do not handle discussing grief openly as an acceptable topic. We feel awkward around it, discomforted as it opens wounds we have not processed and do not want to bring out into the public to discuss. Those of us who are grieving can be shunned, as it is uncomfortable to be around that which reminds us of our own pain. I was touched by how authentic they were about how hard it was to share the very real pain they may be feeling from life's painful realities. They stated exactly what I feel is part of my message about grief; we need to be willing to openly discuss, accept, and acknowledge grief as part of our life experience. We need to help each other through it and embrace it as the deep and profound opportunity it offers for us to truly know ourselves. Grief needs to be brought into our awareness as something important and valuable to understand, learn from, and process in order to heal and be able to move forward in a more mentally and emotionally healthy state of mind. They agreed we do not "do grief" well in our society. It was a very profound discussion. Google it!

My experience is that grief slowly creeps into every part of us, infiltrates our thoughts and feelings, seeps into our emotions and crawls into our hearts. It finds its way into the cells of our body and it takes over how it functions. It finds its way into every aspect of our lives, our relationships, how we respond to the world around us, our behaviors, our perception of life on every level. In time, we can't even recognize ourselves, as grief has taken up residence in who we are.... So I have decided my only option is to make friends with grief since we hang out so much together. I realize it is a lifetime relationship whether I like it or not. Hence, it is a good idea to take steps to get to know my new friend that seems to be influencing so much of who I am now.

If that is the case, I believe to begin healing the emotional impact of grief, we must come to understand it, how it is a new aspect of who we are becoming. To understand it at the core of what grief really is; our emotional response to an ending, something over which we have no control. And we struggle with the acceptance of that permanent change. Therefore it impacts our physical, cognitive, behavioral, social, cultural, spiritual, and philosophical dimensions, depending on the situation and the level of impact. No wonder so many of us are walking wounded from the impact of unresolved grief!

Once we can understand what grief is, we can begin to notice how and where it shows up within us. For there is no healing something if we have not identified the need or existence of it, right? We cannot enter into a process to shift, transform, or evolve the issue interfering in our health and wholeness unless we are aware of its existence, or the need to change whatever is holding us back from thriving. In my case, I think the grief I experienced from Justin's death hit me on every level with a significant impact – a huge tsunami that consumed me in a moment of sudden and unexpected assault. It is clear the body is impacted from an emotional hit just as much as a physical assault. Think about how you have felt under such situations. Energetically, it is like you are jolted out of your body and are watching your body from another place. That is exactly what happened to me. I didn't feel like I was in my body again for many months. That is the numb state – going through motions as if you don't exist because on some level you are not functioning at all. You are not in a state of awareness but in a place of self-observation, and perhaps not consciously. It is watching yourself go through the motions of life as if you are someone else.

In the initial grief state, it is easy to withdraw from normal activities, social connections and just being around people in general. Others can feel uncomfortable too, the elephant in the room no one wants to bring up because it makes them feel awkward. I remember many people saying to me "I feel so bad, I don't know what to say." And I would respond with, "I understand, I feel really bad and don't know what to say either!" It put them at ease because we each had acknowledged there are no words to help relieve the pain of the situation. Even though we naturally want help someone feel better, we can't take their pain away, so we feel helpless. I learned to accept that speaking out was helpful, saying what was real for me in the moment, what was on my heart. I found it was and is the best way to approach sadness, grief, and pain from loss. Allow yourself to be vulnerable in what is authentically happening within you right now, or in the moment grief is welling up within you.

We do that with ease when we are celebrating something, so why not with other situations, as well, especially the more painful and challenging situations? So I now give others permission to share what they want and to let me know if they would rather not talk about something painful at that time. I invite you to come right out and say, "I know this must be painful for you right now, so let me know if you would rather not talk about what is happening with you today (or at this time)." Being genuine, authentic, and compassionate allows most people to respond in the same way; it gives them permission to say what works for them. It is a gift we can provide anyone who is hurting. Or we can offer it ourselves when we are the one experiencing grief, to assist those around us with feeling comfortable speaking to us.

I became very bold in saying what worked for me and what didn't, most of the time. Being human, I did not manage it well all of the time, and still don't. But for the most part, it helped me move through dealing with others as I healed. I became more comfortable talking about my sadness, as it became a more familiar part of me. I tried not to dwell on the source of my pain, but in speaking about how I felt or how I was doing in that moment. To not hide from it. Give it a try and see how it feels to live from your authentic heart. And it is okay to challenge the comfort zone of others; sometimes we need the push to heal what we have hidden deep within us and is hurting us more from not processing it than in speaking to it.

Another thing I have observed from my grief experience is how many others were uncomfortable with my grief, and would rather I got over it so everything could get back to normal, whatever that is. My normal will never be the same again, so the process of grief is as much about learning to be comfortable with what is becoming our new normal. That is why relationships change or end after significant grief happens in life; some people cannot accept our new normal. My new normal may be that I am completely different in how I show up, how I respond to life, what interests me now, or even what I am interested in talking about. Those outside of us may not understand and take it personally. They remain waiting for us to return to the way things were; for us, that will never be an option. The discomfort felt from those outside of you may also be uncomfortable because it triggers their own unresolved grief or memories they are not prepared to deal with in the presence of your fresh grief. Unconsciously, they are rejecting the emotion stirred within them and you represent the discomfort they feel, so they now project onto you the responsibility of making it uncomfortable for them. They would prefer you bury your pain just as they are pushing it deep inside themselves. Awareness of our own grief can assist us in understanding what we are feeling when grief is raw for someone we know and care about, and whom we really want to support.

I actually had the experience of how my grief triggered the response for me to get back to my old normal with a ministry staff member at the time I was in the midst of the grief from my son's murder. Working in a ministry, one would think everyone functions in a high level of understanding and compassion, but we are all human beings doing the best we can to exist in life in any given moment. If we are not intentionally in a state of practicing to do better, be better, grow into a better me, or evolve in some way, we may not be functioning at the level of awareness in all things – who does that 100% of the time? Not me for sure! I know I wasn't functioning at a high level of awareness for a long time after experiencing the level of grief that smacked me out of my body. So when my assistant expected me to get back to normal, and that didn't happen after three or four months, our relationship shifted. I didn't see it coming, though I wasn't looking for it either, but somehow her perspective was I had changed, therefore I was the problem. Her perspective was that after so many months, I should be over talking about my son's murder or still be referring to it in my conversations or even my Sunday lessons. It was uncomfortable for her when I would talk about what happened in my life or reference the impact in any way. But *I was still living it,* still processing it, still figuring out what my new normal was, and completely unsure of what that was supposed to be. I did attempt to be authentic to what was happening within me, how I was processing it, or what I was learning from it as a positive rather than a "woe is me" perspective. But even then, I realized it is not easy for others to hear even a hint of what is present for the one experiencing grief. Our relationship didn't end well, as she resigned several months later, and I am still deeply saddened about that situation today. I don't know if given the circumstances I could have handled it any better, but I can perhaps learn from it and manage it better if in a similar situation in the future. I am holding that intention for myself.

That was my first realization of how others' expectations of our handling grief can impact our relationship and how to manage it day-to-day. We can only decide for ourselves how much to share, or say, or do when we are processing something we have no experience with. Or even if we do, if it is raw in that moment, it will impact our ability to be aware of the impact of others around us. Remember

– those kinds of life experiences are new for us. It is not included in our educational curriculums, nor are they things that happen frequently in our lifetime. So the level of practice is limited, at best. We have no map or guidebook to tell us what is best to do or how to be in any given situation, especially a highly traumatic one. Yes, you can read my book or someone else's research, or go to therapy, but no one knows what will work best for you but you. And no one else can feel what we are feeling within our own bodies. Everything is unique to each person based on our life experiences, education, training, and accumulated knowledge when something tragic happens. We cannot prepare ourselves to know exactly what we will do, or respond as, or know what other people's expectations may be, and in how to manage them as well. So I am wondering, can we all do a little better in supporting each other with all we are exposed to in our lifetime of experiences? Can we be a bit more compassionate, gentle, and open-minded? Ask before we judge, criticize, or condemn? Be willing to approach others with a willingness to understand in a consciousness of love? I know that takes a lot of self-awareness, but in time, practice, and the intention to shift back into awareness and compassion will make a difference in how we navigate the challenges of life and relationships.

I realize that many of us live in the notion that grief is something to get over. I am here to say, if it has not already been made clear, we do not ever get over grief. I will say it again; we do not "get over" grief. The memories of the circumstances that triggered grief will not go away, so we will repeatedly remain vulnerable to triggers. I know that is not what we want to accept, but until we do, we will be blindsided by grief over and over again. Knowing I will experience sadness and emotional pain again around my son's death helps me to prepare for knowing this feeling is going to come around again. And it is something I must learn to manage as I become more comfortable with its impact, using the tools I have put into practice to assist me when grief comes up. The feeling is something I must accept, feel, be present to, and process – again and again. I learn to live with it rather than reject it or bury it. Learning to live with it I thrive. I can move forward intentionally, living a meaningful life using the depth of this new level of awareness of myself to empower my life, rather than diminish it. I can still feel joy and happiness along with the part of me that holds that special pain in the memory of my son. It reminds me of my deep capacity to feel and to love, and that is a true gift!

Pema Chodron, American Zen monk, shares a story about sadness the Dalai Lama originally told in his book, *The Art of Happiness: A Handbook for Living*, in an excerpt from her book, *Getting Unstuck*:

> *"The Dalai Lama was asked if there's anything in his life that he feels bad about. He related a personal story to the co-author about how he was approached by an elderly monk who couldn't do certain yoga poses due to his deteriorated physical condition. The Dalai Lama suggested he not do them; that he was too old. He later found out that this monk had committed suicide, thinking that he would then be reincarnated into a younger body and thus be able to do the exercises.*

> *"So the Dalai Lama was left with regret that he had unintentionally been responsible for this man's death, this man's suicide. The interviewer was stopped in his tracks and said, "Oh, my goodness, how did you ever get rid of that feeling?"*

> *The Dalai Lama paused for quite a long time and he thought about that and then he said, "I didn't. It's still there. I just don't allow it to drag me down and pull me back. I realized that being*

*dragged down or held back by it would be to no one's benefit...
not mine or anybody else's, so I go forward and do the best I can.*

*"We have this idea that we either have it or we get rid of it and
the question came from that point of view ... But there's an ability
to be pierced to the heart by the sorrow of the world and your own
regrets without it dragging you down."*

Understanding what grief is allows us to begin moving forward
knowing it is something all beings experience. And we must learn
to process grief to not only move forward, but also to thrive. The
next step is to acknowledge we are willing to move forward by
going THROUGH it – not around it or under it or tiptoeing into
it or any other way but through it. And we do this so we won't be
dragged down or held back by the impact of our sadness, pain, and
grief. It serves no purpose to live from that state of mind, as the
Dalai Lama stated. We move forward the best we can as we process
the energy of the original source of our pain and sadness, and again
as new pain and sadness comes into our experience throughout our
lifetime.

Human beings have a hard time feeling feelings and emotions.
We tend to avoid going deep into them if at all possible – it's
not comfortable, after all! I know, because I am human and have
recognized that in myself on more than one occasions . . . okay, many
more occasions. Avoidance is the cause of a lot of our problems in
life. Sorry, but that's a reality. And we all do it pretty well. So if we
want to get back to functioning after experiencing something that
triggers grief, we must take the huge and courageous step of feeling
intentionally, and staying with it no matter how uncomfortable it
becomes. The level of discomfort is equal to the level of healing
we are inviting into our experience. This is stated clearly in an
invitation from English author and spiritual teacher Jeff Foster
within a quote from his book *Falling In Love From Where You Are:*

"Perhaps our depression is not a sickness (though I will never argue with anyone who wants to defend that view) but a call to break out, to let go, to lose the old structures and stories we have been holding up about ourselves and the world and rest deeply in the truth of who we really are. Conventional wisdom would have you turn away from melancholy rather than face it. Well-meaning friends and family and self-help gurus may want to fix you, to get you "back to normal," to make you more "positive," whatever that means.

What if the "normal" no longer fits? What if you need to shed your half-shed skin, not climb back into it? What if sadness, and pain, and fear, and all of the waves in life's ocean, just want to move in you, to finally express themselves creatively and not be pushed away?

What if you are not nearly as limited as you were led to believe you were? What if you are vast enough to hold and contain all of life's energies, the "positive" and the "negative?" What if you are beyond both, an ocean of consciousness, unified, boundless and free, in which even the deepest despair has a resting place?

What if your depression was simply you calling yourself back Home, in the only way you knew how?"

Will you accept this invitation to heal, feel, and be free?

EXERCISE: EMOTIONAL FEELING-TO-HEALING SHIFT:

Plan ahead to participate in this exercise. You will want to allow at least 30-45 minutes of quiet, personal, and private time to experience the benefit of feeling deeply and reconnecting to the part of your mind, heart, and soul crying to be released. You may want to have a journal and pen handy to write as you are moved to do so.

Taking a moment to feel means getting comfortable in a place that is nurturing and safe. If you are willing to invite someone to support you, do that. Maybe it is with a coach. Their only role will be sit silently, sending you strength and compassion during the process, then being available to debrief afterward if you desire. This is an exercise I guide people through when they are ready to get back to living from a place of wholeness. You may also play soft instrumental music if that assists you in relaxing and feeling as you connect within. * *To listen to the audio link of the following meditation exercise go to website: www.unityawakeningways.org*

- Begin in your comfortable place with all distractions turned off or shut out. Close your eyes and take a few deep breaths to feel the energy of life moving through you.

- I invite you to now focus on your source of pain, to bring it up into your heart, to see it in your mind; if there is an image that comes with it, go deep into everything it brings up, to really FEEL IT… let the tears flow. Go as deep into the pain as you possibly can!

- Then begin to say what is on your heart out loud or write in a journal, but let all the feelings come crashing out, no matter how ugly and raw they may be, without hesitation, without judgment, without labeling whether they are appropriate, real, valid, correct, or whatever you may call what comes out.

- Are you willing to go there, and then go even deeper? To feel the intensity, not just in your body, but in your words or in what you are writing … all the feelings you have held back and not allowed yourself to let out. Regurgitate it all … throw it up! Get as raw as you can go … cry the ugly cry. *(This is why you would only want someone who accepts you unconditionally without judgment to be present with you, but who also holds sacred space in which you can be vulnerable.)*

Once you feel empty, allow yourself to shift your thoughts to treasured memories and live in those for a while ... Feel the joy, the happiness, the value of those moments, the unconditional love they invoke. Bring them into the focus of your mind with the feelings intensely in your heart. Live in them as if they were happening right now!

- Allow yourself to smile and your heart to swell in the memories that will always live in your heart ... feel the joy as intensely as you felt the pain. Let the memories become a part of you that can never be forgotten or taken from you, forever ingrained within you.

- Write, speak or just be present to each memory that comes up; cherish reliving them....

- And now see the value of that person or circumstance in your life... Ask yourself, "Do the memories in my heart enhance who I am? Do they create an energy that supports and serves me, allows love into my heart? Would I trade them for anything? Can I see how my pain is simply a representation of the level I have loved? Would I want to diminish the level of my love by never having experienced my cherished memories? Would I trade the pain away instead of having the memories I cherish in my heart forever? Answer honestly.

- Let these questions begin to stir a new reality for you. Begin to see how the cherished memories offer you a legacy from what has been lost, from the one you love and who loved you, but is now transformed from the physical form of life. What is that legacy? The legacy is a gift your loved one or lost relationship or belonging is offering you. It may be unconditional love or acceptance or courage or compassion ... something of value you admired in that person or circumstance. Are you willing to accept it? Are you willing to both accept it and use it to enhance your life? To use it to honor the cherished memories and the love you still have?

- Begin to see how you will integrate the legacy gift into your life ... live it in your mind, feel what it feels like in your heart, make it a part of you in this moment ... Now write down what you will do differently using this legacy gift. How will you use it to enhance or change your life? Write it out, consider a possible plan, create steps to take action, and note when you will begin each one. It is important to make a commitment to integrating what you have discerned. Check in with it daily for a while, as you get comfortable integrating this legacy gift from the pain of loss and grief that had been keeping you from moving forward. See how it is shifting your current moments as you embrace it more fully.

- Write out whatever comes to mind, and know that you can go back and re-evaluate it and rework it at any time. You are planting seeds to mature in their own time...

- Make this a part of who you are now, consciously, intentionally, proactively ... affirm it in your mind, claim it in our heart, align it with the intelligence and wisdom already within you...This is the beginning of you becoming your new normal, your enhanced self!

- Can you begin to sense gratitude for this gift? For what this experience of grief has offered you? ... A swelling up within you of appreciation and realization of what an honor it is for your loved one to have left this for you as their legacy gift? Sit with that and become aware of any other aspect it is offering and if you choose to accept it or not, or maybe set it aside for later. As you have the power to choose when, how, why, or not to do...and always have...it is yours to decide.

- Continue writing it until you feel complete … when you do, give yourself a warm hug and congratulate yourself for a job very well done! For this is the beginning of your new and transformed self, enhanced by what grief had to offer you as a legacy from the love that you hold dear, and that will always be a part of who you are…

- Congratulate yourself for having the courage to feel, to heal, and to allow this shift to move you forward. With a SMILE, give thanks for this moment, appreciating the gift received and the new path that is unfolding before you….

CHAPTER 7

SPIRITUAL TEACHINGS ON GRIEF

One of the things I have used in my personal educational and spiritual growth and development is to turn to sacred texts or authors I admire who have shared words of wisdom I value and can see the benefit of incorporating into my life. As a minister and spiritual teacher, I have followed the teachings of Jesus, one I consider a Master Teacher along with Buddha, Lao Tzu, Krishna, and other less known but equally wise teachers and philosophers of life, and many more contemporary authors and spiritual teachers of our more recent timeframe.

Jesus is the most recent of those Master Teachers to have walked the earth, having made a tremendous impact in the world, but also having been very misunderstood by the very religion that claims him as their own. To be clear, Jesus was not a Christian, he was a Jew and never taught what we now call the Bible. He taught from the Jewish Torah, and the Hebrew Bible writings that he would have been familiar with as a Jewish rabbi or teacher. The New Testament is a collection of books written over a period of many decades, the first of which was not written until about 40-50 years after the death of Jesus.

What we teach from the Gospels can only be considered a brief synopsis of what Jesus may have taught, as there were no reporters going around writing down everything he said. In the era of Jesus, information was shared orally and therefore would have changed based on the interpretation or purpose of the one who shared it. We know how stories get changed over time, so we can only guess to the real core essence of his teachings. And we know many texts written during the time after Jesus's death were not preserved or canonized in the Bible. What was included in the Bible has been documented to have been decided on by the Council of Rome in around 382CE.

The council then chose only what was considered important based on their concept of what was relevant to them and what they wanted people to base Christian religious philosophy on; therefore much was lost in that process. As a matter of fact, any writings not included in the final canonization of the Bible were intentionally destroyed so as not to create alternative teachings. Though, fortunately, many were preserved and discovered hidden thousands of years later with what is now known as the Nag Hammadi Library, or Gnostic Gospels, as they are sometimes referred to, found near the Upper Egyptian town of Nag Hammadi in 1945. The discovered texts included the Book of Thomas, which contains many quotations attributed to be from Jesus himself.

Scholars believe that if we only had the Beatitudes, shared in the Books of Matthew and Luke in what has come to be known as *The Sermon on the Mount,* and what we call *The Lord's Prayer,* we would have the core teachings of what Jesus' message contained. Each one is a lesson or affirmation of Truth that holds meaning and value if used as a guide in our life. And of course we will never have the full meaning and intention of what he may have said because of the many translations the original texts have gone through, ultimately changing what the meaning may have been when spoken from Jesus' lips. If we do not understand the culture and meaning of the original language, we lose the fullness of what the teaching may have intended. I have found seeking a truer interpretation can bring a deeper meaning of Jesus' teaching, thus making them practical in today's reality. For if not practical and applicable, what purpose do they serve? The one I have turned to for support with grief is the well-known Beatitude *"Blessed are those who mourn, for they shall be comforted."* It speaks to me in ways that say "listen to this, it offers you what you need to move through your pain…." The value and the gift in Jesus' message is that it has direct and relevant meaning for our life in any era. It is practical and important, providing a way to support us in whatever we need in this moment of life right now. For Jesus came to show us the way – in fact, his teachings were called "The Way" in the early days after his death, not Christianity. The first reference to "Christians" in the Bible is from Acts, Chapter 11 where it says, *"the disciples were called Christians first in Antioch."* This was the place the first church was started and disciples were taught. So if we see teachings of Jesus as deep universal ways to live, as guidance to live by, then we can see the significant value they offer to transform our reality in even today's world!

I have turned to Dr. Rocco A. Errico, an ordained minister, international lecturer and author, spiritual counselor, and one of the nation's leading Biblical scholars, working from the original Aramaic Peshitta texts. His deep understanding of the Aramaic language provides a way for us to gain a new insight into what Jesus' teachings offer and how to apply them in practical ways into our current culture and way of living. Dr. Errico helps us realize that not every Aramaic (or Greek) word translates directly into our English language with the same meaning and intent we may use in our current lifestyle. And when translated from Aramaic or Greek into German and then English it loses another layer or layers of original meaning and intent. When researching and exploring the meaning of "Blessed are those who mourn…" I came to understand that it had a direct implication to the meaning and value of grief. Thank you, Dr. Rocco Errico!

We have no further to search than to take this "Beatitude" and use it to move through our pain and loss experience of grief, and to begin to unravel it to understand how it offers us comfort and guidance in the process of healing and transformation. First I want to clarify that "Beatitude" can be translated into something more like a blessing, but with great joy, or "happy as", so it is with great joy this information is offered and it is with great joy I receive it! It is just what I need now and I will have the courage to use it, and live by it – to intentionally receive it as valuable and relevant.

I know the concept to be "blessed" because I am mourning what may seem like a conflict of emotion, but the word 'mourn' means more than feeling sadness; it invites us to seek a deeper place for healing. From Jesus' language it means more significantly to go deep into feeling the pain and grief from loss, to be willing to feel it all, to go deep into it … seeking to know more of what it can offer us, to discover a gift within it somehow. It is saying, "let us seek to know God in this experience, for God – the source of all life, the very vibration of my soul, is waiting for me to reach out for comfort and support and is available to me now. Am I willing to go there? To seek a deeper relationship with the Divine living within me? Am I willing to use my pain, my sorrow, my grief, to transform me at a deep and profound level?"

This is what Jesus is saying, seek and then seek more, be blessed by this transformational experience. And then you will know the Kingdom, the very sanctuary of your soul, the place where God is; the place where we access comfort, wisdom, truth, and divine guidance. What better place to be than in the place where God is when we are hurting? When we are in such pain we cannot see where our next step should be or if we can even move forward in any direction at all.

The comfort, the willingness, the blessing, the gift, the ability to use this loss to become more of who I truly am, is the reward in setting out on this journey of grief. To seek to mourn, to go deep into the comfort only the Divine can offer us. I know I would never have chosen this path intentionally, nor would any of you, I believe, and Jesus understood that about our human nature. He also understood it is a part of our human experience we cannot escape. So he offered us the understanding that life will be painful at times, things will happen, we will experience loss, painful loss, and it is in those times we can choose to use the energy of that pain to go deep within ourselves to know what we have been seeking all along, a connection with God. Or by whatever name we call the source of all life – the mysterious indescribable creative essence that forms life. It matters not what we name it. It does matter that we seek it, to experience and embrace it, and to accept all that energy offers us as we choose to align with it. It is in the very breath we breathe, something we are never without until we cease to exist in our present physical form. Though we may not continue to "breathe" the air of this earthly reality, we transition into another form that carries with it the energy of our divine essence available to us in spirit.

Dr. Errico also interpreted the Aramaic definitions of the words "*mourn*" and "*comfort*" collectively to mean "*grace*." So on another level, this Beatitude suggests that one who turns to Godness – the essence of God within us – in any kind of distress or unhappiness will receive comfort, meaning guidance, direction, and support, because we were willing to seek it.

From this teaching, to *mourn* is to confront life, the pain, the presenting loss – our own and the pain of the world that can trigger unresolved grief – and it calls on us to take action. It calls on us to contribute to what is lacking and align it with Godness, which in turn creates comfort that directly results in making a difference in our own life and in the consciousness of humanity. That is *grace*; something that is beyond our own understanding or creation. Despite ourselves, there is divine support available to us if we turn within and make the effort to connect to it.

Charles Fillmore was the co-founder of the Unity Movement begun in 1889 as part of the resurgence of New Thought Spirituality that has had a tremendous impact on our spiritual teachings of today. He wrote a book called *The Revealing Word*, which is sort of a dictionary of New Thought definitions of spiritually used words. In it, he defines "*grace*" this way: "*Good will; favor; disposition to show mercy; aid from God in the process of regeneration.*" This means that despite the law of cause and effect, we will always reap more than we sow, because the very act of reaching out brings more than an equal share of results into our manifest reality. The well-known Parable of the Prodigal Son is a prime example of *grace* found in the book of Luke 15:11-32. If the farmer's son had not taken the first step toward changing his life and asking for forgiveness, a step toward his own healing, his life would have continued to spiral down into an even more miserable existence of pain and suffering. And he did not have to travel all the way to the front doorstep on his own. Before he made it all the way home, his father ran out to warmly greet him by throwing his arms around him in welcome and love, no questions asked. He did not have to make the journey entirely on his own, he was recognized and accepted as one who belonged all along – that is grace, meeting us before we have had to make the whole journey by ourselves, without having had to make 100% of the effort. The process of "*grace*," according to Charles

Fillmore, is" *the influence or spirit of God operating in humans to regenerate or strengthen them.*" When we seek to know the Godness within – to *"mourn,"* we automatically connect with that which strengthens us and transforms the pain that is preventing us from living fully, our comfort.

I believe Jesus is saying to us, "Blessed are those who have experienced terrible losses" because those terrible losses can become extraordinary paradigm shifters – the process of transformation. These losses will challenge us to change our thinking; to open us to new behaviors, new practices, new world realities. We are being invited to live in a new world based on this crisis, this painful experience, this horrendous loss. But we will need to go through the grieving process if we are to embrace this new paradigm, this new world reality. We must acknowledge what has been lost. We must acknowledge who we are in this circumstance, the decisions that we made or did not make, all the variables contained in the situation. And at the same time, the universe is inviting us to become much bigger than we ever thought we could possibly be… through this mourning process. It is a journey of courage, willingness, acceptance, and forgiveness. It is a journey we must be willing to enter into if we are to truly find the way through to the other side of it and receive the benefit, the blessing, the gift. The *"comfort"* offered will become the guidance and wisdom necessary to embrace our new life fully and discover the deeper meaning it has always offered us. Grief became the push we need to take us there.

So perhaps we can rephrase this Beatitude in this way: *"Happy are those whose identity is so shaken that they can begin to discover that part of themselves that can never be shaken and now knows the way forward."* And, Grief can really shake us up – right? That is its job. That's why it exists in our human experience. If we were not shaken up along the way, we would never seek to become the potential that resides within us from the moment of our first breath.

When I sat with this Beatitude after exploring what it may really mean as a lesson of value in my life, I began to realize the gift in my willingness to "*mourn*," to go deep into my feelings, to tap into my emotions and seek the comfort of the Godness within me to soothe my broken, shaken heart. Then when I was ready, it would begin to lead me through to the other side of healing and the beginning of the transformed me into the new world reality already existing for me. Something stirred within me that said, "Yes," I am willing to get through the intensity of my pain to receive the gift of whatever it has for me to accept; to become what I am ready to be in my newly transforming self. I had to be willing to take the first step toward my healing though, to experience grace.

> *"It isn't what happens to us that causes us to suffer; it's what we say to ourselves about what happens."*
> ~ **Pema Chodron**

It is in the process of becoming my transformed self that I realized that no matter what has happened in our lives, in my life, even those things like the death of my son that impacted me so significantly, that shook me to my core; my self-talk and how I choose to move forward will have the greatest impact on my personal healing and my ability to move forward to thrive. Thriving is something we are meant to experience on the highest vibrational level of life. Thriving is another form of 'to be blessed'.

> *"There is a story of a woman running away from tigers. She runs and runs and the tigers are getting closer and closer. When she comes to the edge of a cliff, she sees some vines there, so she climbs down and holds on to the vines. Looking down, she sees that there are tigers below her as well. She then notices that a mouse is*

gnawing away at the vine to which she is clinging. She also sees a beautiful little bunch of strawberries close to her, growing out of a clump of grass. She looks up and she looks down. She looks at the mouse. Then she just takes a strawberry, puts it in her mouth, and enjoys it thoroughly. Tigers above, tigers below. This is actually the predicament that we are always in, in terms of our birth and death. Each moment is just what it is. It might be the only moment of our life; it might be the only strawberry we'll ever eat. We could get depressed about it, or we could finally appreciate it and delight in the preciousness of every single moment of our life".

~ Pema Chödrön, The Wisdom of No Escape: How to Love Yourself and Your World

I had reached the place where I could begin to feel gratitude for even my pain, for my grief, as I would not have been willing to go that deep into my heart and soul otherwise. I would not have been willing to allow the Divine in me to transform what needed to change for me to take a step toward realigning with my Wholeness. Wholeness is the place we live when we are completely expressing from our Divine Nature, our Godness; the place we exist when we are free from dis-ease in mind, body, soul, and are healed. Healing is not the elimination of what appears to be broken, not functioning as we expect or expressing sickness, it is in lifting up our vibrational energy to align with our Divinity, our True Self. Wholeness is our birthright and the true demonstration of who we are. It is what we are to be seeking in every experience life offers. In our seeking, we find comfort and the tranquil place where we discover Truth and wisdom within.

I ask you now, "Are you ready to be blessed through the process of mourning, to be shaken so dramatically that you will begin to discover your true identity? So you may experience the comfort, healing and guidance of Spirit – the part of you who can never be shaken? To be transformed at depth, to be renewed in mind, heart, body and soul?" It is only when we can say "yes" that we begin the healing process and realize that grief has something valuable to offer, as a gift we never knew existed. Acceptance of what is begins the way ... and "yes" is the practice.

CHAPTER 8

UNRAVELING GRIEF: STEPS TO CLAIMING NEW MEANING

"We think that the point is to pass the test or overcome the problem, but the truth is that things don't really get solved. They come together and they fall apart. Then they come together again and fall apart again. It's just like that. The healing comes from letting there be room for all of this to happen: room for grief, for relief, for misery, for joy."
~ Pema Chödrön, When Things Fall Apart: Heartfelt Advice for Hard Times

Something I know now after years living the most profound grief experience of my life, is that I can say I am grateful for having had grief challenge me to my core, to have shaken me in a way I could not ignore. And also for stretching me to become more than I may have been willing to step into because of it. Not that I am grateful my son was taken from me in such a horrific way, for I will never stop yearning for him or wishing he were still with me in the physical, but that I was given this opportunity to go deep into my soul and know myself more profoundly. To know the path to experience our Godness is one that takes a courageous leap into the unknown without hesitation, allowing whatever is being revealed to be used for greater good. Not the good that is the opposite of bad, but the good that represents the creative flow of life within me being used for a greater expression in and through and as me.

When we can shift our thinking from "it has to feel good," or "be only what I want" or "what is my interpretation of success," we can begin to accept everything life presents and decide how we will either use it, ignore it, transform it, or release it. For everything does serve a purpose, whether we realize it or not, whether we like it or not. What I am practicing, to the best of my ability in any given moment, is to live from a place of awareness, openness, and curiosity in life. When we experience anxiety, fear, anger, or pain as a result of something that has happened, we immediately are removed from awareness, openness, and curiosity. We retract our energy into our limited human nature responses of survival or protection and are no longer receptive to the limitless possibilities from our Divine Nature. And that means all those things we have yet to consider, think of, or realize the existence of. It is natural to be anxious or unsure when stepping into a new situation or unfamiliar experience (and that is where we live with grief, an unfamiliar experience), but with awareness we can recognize this feeling and consciously shift into the place of observation. This is the place where we can decide what our next move will be, our next choice – or not to choose. We can decide to get drawn into the fear, drama, unforgiveness, or anger in the moment or take a deep breath, center into our heart space and ask, "How shall I respond? What is my best action?" And it could be to do nothing for now. To wait, seek, research more, gather more information before deciding anything. That applies to every situation or experience we encounter – the "take a breath before moving into action" concept.

STEPS TO CLAIMING NEW MEANING THROUGH GRIEF:

STEP 1 – Take Time To Be and Listen

In the early experience of grief and loss, taking time to be and to listen to that gentle voice within is the best form of self-support we can choose. And if we must, to do nothing other than the required actions to take care of life. Take time to just be with your feelings, emotions, and thoughts, to observe and watch them. That is the "seeking into mourning" process. The beginning of going deep into our personal relationship with God, or our source or the vibration of life, whatever you may call that deep connection with your divine self, that sense of Godness within. There is no rushing or set amount of time it should take. It is whatever time serves you.

Marianne Williamson said, "*I surrender it to God, knowing that the pain itself is a product or a reflection of how I am interpreting whatever it is that is causing me pain. Some pain is simply the normal grief of human existence. That is pain I try to make room for. I honor my grief. I try to be kinder to myself. I give myself time to move through and to process whatever is making me sad.*" ~ From "A Conversation with Marianne Williamson: Powerful pioneer in new thought and spirituality". Interview with Maranda Pleasant, www.marandapleasantmedia.com.

So let me encourage you to get used to listening to your heart and what it is telling you. It will let you know when to move into the next step along this path. To let you know when to stop and feel, to listen, or do something. We get better at listening and relating to our inner GPS with practice. We get better at recognizing its voice and how to differentiate it from an outside influence or from our inner divine wisdom. Once we know our inner voice, it becomes very distinguishable and clear. We will stop doubting ourselves and be more courageous in how we embrace life. Grief can teach us this practice. *To listen to the audio link of the following meditation exercise go to website: www.unityawakeningways.org*

A LISTENING MEDITATION PRACTICE:

Have a journal handy to write your reflections when complete.

- Take time to sit still, without distraction, in a quiet and comfortable space.

- If you are not using the audio recording, and if it would enhance this time for you, play quiet meditative music to relax you.

- With eyes closed, feet flat on the floor and hands gently on your lap with palms open to receive, focus on your breathing.

- Let your mind focus on your inhale and exhale breaths, breathing deeply and slowly with each flow.

- After several minutes of simply breathing, shift your mind to noticing what you feel. Simply observe whatever it is. Notice where in your body you feel what you are feeling.

- Ask what you feel if there is something it wants you to know? Listen to the voice within. Refrain from forcing a "voice," but see if your feelings are conveying a message for you to realize from simply listening with your thoughts, emotions, and feelings. What is forming from this listening?

- Now ask if there is something you need to be doing to support your healing? And again, listen. Listen from your whole being to what comes through, without judgment.

- Finally, simply sit in the silence of your being affirming, "I am open and receptive to whatever it is I need to know...." Without judgment or thinking what it "should" be, listen with an open mind to receive for as long as you feel moved to listen.

- After it feels like the inner voice is complete, take a few deep breaths of thankfulness. Express inner appreciation for whatever was received.

- Open your eyes and write down what you experienced and what you know is valuable to capture as useful. Be in a space of gratitude as you write.

-

STEP 2 – What To Release & What Offers Value?

To be in a place of embracing life is where we want to be in the end of our initial grief process. To unravel all its moving parts and spend time exploring what they have to offer us, releasing what no longer is useful, and integrating what offers value. Ask yourself the following questions and record them in your journal:

- What things are no longer useful to me now?

  - Things that may no longer be useful are resentment, victim consciousness, unforgiveness, anger, fear, self-doubt or unworthiness, negativity, feeling overwhelmed, hopelessness, frustration to name a few.

- What things offer value to me at this moment in time?

  - Things that may offer value are strength, love, compassion, courage, willingness, forgiveness, curiosity, peacefulness, balance, acceptance, gratitude, perseverance, positive thoughts, and so on.

STEP 3 – Recognizing the Gift

"What we have once enjoyed we can never lose. All that we love deeply becomes a part of us".
~ Helen Keller

The next step is to initiate the process of transforming the energy of grief by taking time to recognize the gifts that are a result of what we have lost in the physical, but are offered to us as something of value that enhances our lives.

Take some meaningful time to consider by answering the following questions:

(It may be similar to the exercise in Chapter 6, but be open to applying this exercise to go deeper into the value of the gift within your grief experience, you may use some of the insight from that exercise to begin with this deeper process. Translate "loved one" to whatever identifies your loss or cause of pain – the process is the same no matter what the source of pain.)

- How did my loved one live their life? Is there something in how they approached life, or provided me as a model that I can use to enhance my experience in life now? Write down what comes to you, it is their gift to you.

- What gift is my grief offering me? The legacy of what is offered or what the gift(s) represent? Just write what comes up, there are no wrong answers.

- Then close your eyes and feel the gift as part of you. How does it feel to be one with it? Write it down.

- How will it enhance your life in a way that makes a difference now that you recognize the gift for what it is? Write it down.

- How will you integrate it into your life now? Write it down. Give it a date to take action with specific steps you will take. Consider simple action steps at this point; a more detailed exercise follows.

Taking time to accept and appreciate the legacy gifts our loved one/s or lost situation has left us provides us with a tool we can use to enhance who we are or our life reality. It becomes the energy that propels us into making that paradigm shift into moving forward to thrive. It is almost like realizing a treasured last will and testament has been left for us to pick up and enhance our life as the missing piece we never knew we needed. The most meaningful and valuable part of what we miss the most is left for us to integrate into who we are becoming. Celebrate that!

When I considered what Justin's life represented for me, I began to see him through a different lens. To see his life and the way he lived as a rare gift I would not have accepted or used unless this separation of living in two different planes of existence had manifested. Thinking about Justin, I began to realize he offered me fearlessness, to live boldly as if there may be no tomorrow, to leave nothing for chance but to go for it; to be courageous and live in the moment. WOW, his legacy to me was so powerful I almost could not contain its fullness at first conception. But he did live life on the edge, even in his little chubby baby days; he was curious and explored without fear or timidly holding back. Thus the many hospital emergency room visits, the climbing to the outer edge of tree limbs to see how far he could go before they would break, or to go sky diving and want to do it over and over again, or driving fast and dreaming of being a race car driver. There was an inner voice in my head that had been calling me to *"fly free"* for years, but I had not truly embraced that freely until I realized Justin's legacy to me was to finally make it part of how I lived life now. It was time for me accept Justin's legacy to live on the edge but with balance and openness to explore beyond the boundaries of my own self-limited reality. If I refuse, I devalue what his life represented and his gift would forever remain hidden and meaningless. I would never want that to happen.

Take a moment to live in the life of who or what you grieve and consider the legacy it offers you as the gift that will keep the treasured memories alive through you. Identify the gift that will enhance who you are becoming as a result of having grieved the memory of those whom you love. Write whatever it is down and claim it – things like courage, compassion, adventurous heart, kindness, faith, strength, wisdom, perseverance, or peacefulness ... Perhaps create a special representation of the gift(s) as a constant reminder of the treasured gift that was the authentic last will and testament left just for you, should you choose to accept it.

STEP 4 – Creating Meaning As Legacy

Once we have realized the legacy gift from who or what we grieve, we are in the place where we can begin to consider how we want to move forward as the enhanced version of who I have become. For in this process of unraveling grief, we eventually reach the step where we decide how we will move forward.

Ask yourself:

- What new meaning will I add to the life I am now creating?

    Coming to terms with the fact that I am no longer the person I was before this experience of grief entered my life, I must come to realize that my life needs to be re-evaluated. To consider how I have been living, and how do I want to live from now on?

- What changes do I want to make or need to make to be authentic to who I am now, that I have integrated the legacy provided for me from my loved one's life? (Or lost value)

    Because I am not in the same mold I was previously, I may not fit in the life I have been living. As a result of accepting the legacy gift that was left for me, I realize I must now consider choosing what needs to change, to be enhanced, or shifted, or released, or added into my life. What is that?

- What will provide the new meaning and purpose of the new life I am creating for myself now?

So we are offered a time to explore the deep questions of the heart to courageously begin implementing what will be the living legacy I offer to those I leave behind some day. When we accept we are literally living our own legacy, we begin to observe our life in new and meaningful ways. It takes on a whole new perspective. This is another empowering gift offered from taking this deep and profound journey of grief – the gift keeps on giving when we live a life of meaning and intentionally living our legacy.

- Begin to ask yourself: What goals, visions, and heart desires are seeking to be activated in my life now?

- Now that I have prepared a stronger foundation built on my profound transformational grief experience, what will I begin adding to my life?

- What will I release or choose to change in order for those things to manifest? (See Step 2 for considerations)

This can be a fun and creative time that is a surprising bonus gift of grief. Again, I did not see that coming, and maybe it is not what you would expect either, but it is part of the transformational healing process of deep grief. This is an opportunity to reinvent your life, your behaviors, your actions, what you will or will not do. This is a time to get the clarity that can enhance our life experience in more meaningful and creative ways – if we take conscious and intentional time to go deep within to tap into what is waiting to come forth in and through and as you. This is a time to be grateful for the life that inspired you to become more than you had dared to be before. Honor yourself and your loved one by not letting your legacy be lost in the pain of loss. Use it to create something new and beautiful!

EXERCISE TO REINVENT YOUR LIFE:

Give yourself an hour or more to begin; it may be something you do over several weeks or more. There is no rush to reinventing your life; just stay focused on creating the content and steps to implement change.

Tools to gather before you begin: pen/pencil, journal or notebook to record your responses.

1) Consider now without judging, or figuring out the how or why, or the details or if anyone else will approve, what you would love to be creating, doing, or being?

2) Look at all areas of your life and make note of what is being called to change, create, or do for each one in a separate column or sheet of paper: health and wholeness, career or life participation, relationships, and spirituality.

Note: There may be subareas under each. Write them down and just list what the new description is for each one under the primary category.

Be bold, not the "easy to make happen" things, but the deep "what if" things I have never been brave enough to consider. Be outrageously wild!

3) Then sit with each and try it on – take your time with each one:

- How does it feel?
- What does it look like with YOU in it?

- What are you doing or being in each new area? Vividly experience it in your mind, making it as real as possible to get a full taste, sense of smell, the sounds, and the physical sensations involved.

Write down what comes up for you while observing and living in each area. Use the listening practice to receive clarity on each concept as you go deep into considering how you want to reinvent that part of your life. Listen to what it has to share with you.

- You may want to just focus on one area at a time over a week or more before moving on to another. Honor what you feel guided to work on and when.

4) Next, consider what you may need to release in order for those things to happen. Write down for each area what is in the way of that item from happening – focusing on each area as you are ready:

- A rigid thought?
- A behavior that needs changing to allow you to be or do something different?
- A job or relationship change?
- A fixed position that keeps you stuck?
- An attitude that cannot fully embrace this idea?
- What would offer you freedom by shifting, changing, or releasing something, to engage, express or experience this desired action?

Just note what is realized; not that you will do it yet, just that you recognize value in releasing, changing, or shifting those things. Again, you may want to just focus on one item at a time.

5) Now sit with each item and the awareness of what may need to be released for the desired result to happen – the newly identified items from above.

- How does it feel to release or change those things?

- Write it down. It is important to recognize something needs to shift in order to claim what you want to be doing or expressing differently.

- Now ask yourself how would it feel to manifest the result of the desired item? Write that down. Knowing how it would feel begins to make it real within you. The beginning of allowing it to manifest change as you.

6) ASK for each item in each area as you are working on them:

- *Is the desire* to implement this new thing into your life *greater than* any *fear or concern* to release what is in its way from *successful results?*

- If the desire is greater, circle it as something you will create in your life. It has become a goal to be achieved.

- Write down a date you would like to have it complete by - it can be updated later if new information is realized, but allow yourself a realistic goal date to make it firm in written form to validate your commitment.

7) **Create a Legacy Vision List** – on a separate page, list each goal by category and prioritize each one. Know you are creating a living legacy; this process may be a year or more in manifesting depending on the number of areas you are reinventing! One thing at a time will manifest a new and more meaningful life.

Then take a moment to consider:

- Is there is anything that comes up different from what you already realized? It may need to be released from each vision area before, so note on a new page or under your Vision List: **What needs to be released to live my vision list.** Add anything you recognize as something of value to *be released* on this list, specific to each goal. Prioritize the order you will work on releasing under each goal. These are important things to consciously eliminate from your thinking, words, or use, actions or behaviors you engage in to allow for the energy they hold to be transformed from preventing the creative energy to manifest your living vision.

For each item to be released:

- Decide *when* you will begin releasing each item from your list with a bold affirmation of completion: "I now release_____! I am grateful for having released_____!"

- Next to each item, write an affirmation claiming what you are replacing that item with. "I now claim this new expression, thought process, behavior or action_____, I am grateful for manifesting this empowering new expression within me, beginning today _____!

- Spend time each day with one item. If you feel you are not complete with the one you focused on the day before, continue claiming release and affirming the new expression until it feels authentic to you before beginning the next one. Remember, there is no timeframe to do this "right;" it is not a race to the finish line. It is a life process I am authentically engaged in to make deep and powerful transformational change within me. It would be appropriate to take three to six weeks for each item or more – until a new norm is conditioned within you.

- Journal the thoughts and feeling that come up during this process. Pay attention to new ideas or concepts of how to move forward becoming, implementing, or practicing the affirmative action of living your legacy. Then courageously take the action necessary to implement this intention into motion.

- See how day-by-day your life takes form in new and abundant ways. Choose each day to step into who you are and how you will show up intentionally one powerful action at a time as you live your legacy of life.

A FABLE: CARROTS, EGGS, OR COFFEE

A young woman went to her grandmother and told her about her life and how things were so hard for her. She did not know how she was going to make it and wanted to give up. She was tired of fighting and struggling. It seemed that as one problem was solved, a new one would pop up.

Her grandmother took her to the kitchen. She filled three pots with water and placed each on a high fire, and soon the pots came to boil. In the first pot she placed carrots, in the second she placed eggs, and in the last she placed ground coffee beans. She let them sit and boil; without saying a word. In about twenty minutes, she turned off the burners. She fished the carrots out and placed them in a bowl. She pulled the eggs out and placed them in a bowl. Then she ladled the coffee out and placed it in a bowl.

Turning to her granddaughter, she asked, "Tell me what you see."

"Carrots, eggs, and coffee," she replied. Her grandmother brought her closer and asked her to feel the carrots. She did and noted that they were soft. The grandmother then asked the granddaughter to take an egg and break it. After pulling off the shell, she observed the hard-boiled egg. Finally, the grandmother asked the granddaughter to sip the coffee. The granddaughter smiled as she tasted its rich aroma, then asked,

"What does it mean, grandmother?"

Her grandmother explained that each of these objects had faced the same adversity: boiling water. Each reacted differently. The carrot went in strong, hard, and un-relenting. However, after being subjected to the boiling water, it softened and became weak. The egg had been fragile. Its thin outer shell had protected its liquid interior, but after sitting through the boiling water, its inside became hardened. The ground coffee beans were unique, however. After they were in the boiling water, they had changed the water.

"Which are you?" she asked her granddaughter.

This story has rich meaning when applied to our lives. Grief can be like the boiling water that has the potential to change us at depth. But we can choose how we will allow the impact on who we are to be changed. So ask yourself, "Which are you?" How you choose to live your life legacy will be the outer realization of your choice. Consider from a place of deep awareness and contemplation how you will allow grief to change you. *Not if* grief will change you because *it will* change you. You can decide if it will change you unconsciously without your input, or if you will use it as the rich and empowering gift it offers to be enhanced and transformed just as a chrysalis becomes a butterfly. Grief enters into the process of our lives because it has no choice, but instead of fighting the process or resisting it, we can embrace it to become the unique and beautiful expression it was divinely designed to become within us. That can be you. We are all butterflies waiting to be released to fly freely! Grief can be our catalyst.

Grief will always live as part of you now, but it will be up to you to choose how it defines you and how well you use it to live a meaningful life because of it. Move forward with a new meaning for life, fully conscious of the legacy you are living each day starting today.

CHAPTER 9

SIBLING GRIEF IMPACT

"Brothers aren't simply close; brothers are knit together."
~ Robert Rivers

I asked my firstborn son, Ryan, to share his thoughts about losing his brother. I realize that the impact of grief on a sibling can be just as significant as on a parent, as siblings have a special relationship that is different from parent/child. I have read that siblings are often swept under the carpet, so to speak, as the parents get the most attention in the sorrow of loss. Siblings are often thought to have more strength and the ability to hold the family together during the grieving process and their feelings can easily get pushed aside and not recognized as just as deep, just as painful, just as impactful on their lives.

I also realize there is survivor's guilt that can easily become a part of a sibling's grief experience. Survivor's guilt can lead to thoughts or the act of suicide, so is important to be recognized in supporting the healing of grief when someone has lost a sibling. Their hearts are hurting deeply and may not be able to voice or feel they can voice the level of grief felt in such a loss. I know my older son felt a sense of responsibility for his younger brother and that he had let him down somehow by not being there to prevent what happened to him. I am sure, though, that he knows logically he could not have been there for every occurrence in Justin's life. But in the moment of realizing what has happened, our minds go to "How could I have prevented this?" I know; my mind did that. So just as for a parent, speaking from my own experience, it can feel like a piece of their heart has been lost forever. And like anyone experiencing the pain of loss through grief, they are forever changed.

I hope, Ryan, that I supported you in a way that provided you with comfort and space to grieve as we navigated this life-changing experience together. I will always remember the very touching moment when we embraced after Justin's memorial was finished and we were looking out at the water along Agate Pass, as we sobbed into each other's arms. The raw emotion of what we felt and shared was a perfect release of the pain we mutually had been carrying for a month up to that day. Feeling your vulnerability to let your feelings go gave me permission to let go all the pent-up pain in my heart with you. I treasure that moment we had together even through the pain that was present at the time.

When the first defendant in Justin's murder case came up for parole in April 2018, Ryan was allowed to share a written statement on how his brother's death impacted his life, which I read on his behalf at the hearing. I feel his words, like the portion of my statement I shared at the beginning of this book, reflect the impact to his heart, mind, and physical-life reality. The depth of his relationship with his brother and the significance of his loss is felt through his words. I tear up every time I read the profound impact his brother's death had on every aspect of his life.

I believe that sharing Ryan's voice reflects the magnitude of how the single act of a few individuals impacted a life so significantly. He was forever changed, like a part of him was ripped out and left as a gaping wound; he had no ability to sew it back together. His point is made, the impact felt, and his raw feelings around what the consequence of those responsible for his brother's death should be without holding back. This is the voice of grief at its core:

"I have thought a lot about what I'd say in a letter, yet the words keep escaping me. My brother was my best friend. My earliest memory. The only consistent friend I had while growing up. And you took him. You decided it was your right to take him away. From his brother. From his mother. From his father. From his friends, who loved him like he was their own brother. From his daughter. You took a little girl's father away from her. Forever. So many people loved Justin, so many people's lives were torn apart the day you decided it was your choice to end his. I went into a two-year tailspin, with relationships destroyed, and depression overtaking every part of my life. I have days where the pain of missing him is unbearable. I wake up at night thinking about him, still to this day. I feel the pain of his loss as if it was yesterday. My every waking thought was for you to pay for what you did. You do not deserve forgiveness. You do not deserve pity. You do not deserve compassion. You deserve to spend the rest of your life in prison. You took everything from him, and ruined countless more lives in the process. You don't deserve anything in this life but anguish and sorrow. I plead with the court to not grant any parole. The pain that has been caused by this senseless act goes beyond any rehabilitation. A good man, a good father, and a good brother was taken too early. Justin was loved by every single person he crossed paths with. He was a special one. A person that would take another's life in that fashion is not a person with a soul. He should not have a second chance at life. He already took one."

My heart yearns to wrap my arms around my son every time I realize the depth of his pain from the loss of his brother. He lives across the country from me now, so I wrap my arms around him in my mind and when we find ourselves in the same place at the same time, I hug him in person. My sons were close as brothers; they shared things I was never a part of, a special connection. This grief journey takes on many levels of impact and each person connected to the loss is affected individually based on their relationship, foundation of ability to handle trauma, life education, and experiences. I am realizing more and more as I step deeper into my journey that honoring each member of the family and including each other in ways to heal and transform the pain felt is important. Take time to talk about the cherished memories of the one you have loved and lost. Laugh and cry together. Let each one know they are loved and can share what is on their heart at any time – keep the love connection open and flowing. Take time to be with each other; do not let special moments get away from you. For it is very sad to live with regret for not spending time with someone who matters when you could have. I know from my experience that regret is part of the grieving process as our minds naturally go to how we could have had more time now that it is seemingly lost. Taking time to do those things with those who are still here will allow each of you to move forward by honoring your relationship and finding new meaning in the life each of you still have to live.

> *"The only people who think there's a time limit for grief have never lost a piece of their heart. Take all the time you need."*
> - Familyfriend poems online

CHAPTER 10

LIVING A LIFE AS GRATITUDE

"Gratitude makes sense of our past, brings peace for today, and creates a vision for tomorrow."
~ Melody Beattie

"I Embrace Changes In Life As Blessings."

"When an oyster suffers irritation from a foreign body in its shell, it responds by secreting more shell-making substance. The intruder is not cast out but enfolded, coated by layers of what is called mother of pearl as it is gradually transformed into a smooth and precious pearl. Like the oyster, I choose to see irritations as invitations to make pearls! I release resistance and accept any such experience as part of life. As I enfold the situation in love, I see how temporary life challenges lose their power to annoy and become gifts. As I bless each challenge, I allow it to help me find the peace of God within. Gratefully, I magnify the treasures of the kingdom."
(Above reprinted with permission of Unity®, publisher of Daily Word)

"So if anyone is in Christ, there is a new creation: everything old has passed away; see, everything has become new!"
~ *2 Corinthians 5:17 NRSV*

Blessings in life are the moments of gratitude that come out of seeming loss, an irritation or painful experience that were not obvious at the time. And often times, the process of moving through the experience results in something unexpected, meaningful, and valuable. It is about allowing the very essence of what a moment in time offers us as it rises up to the surface, sharing its potential, blessing us with the vibration of life. That is how I view the gift of gratitude that comes into our reality out of the human experience of grief. Something new is being born into who and what we are becoming out of the most painful moments of life. Are we courageous enough to seek it out? To see it for what it is?

Understanding gratitude is important in our grief journey. Why? For with gratitude, people can acknowledge the goodness in their lives even in the face of loss, tragedy, or pain. Gratitude helps us feel more positive feelings and emotions, to cherish the happy or good experiences by recognizing their value more because of the moment of pain from loss. Gratitude actually improves our health and by expressing it, our mental, physical, and relational well-being is enhanced! Gratitude assists us in dealing with adversity, and can be the foundation of building strong relationships.

It is interesting that according to the dictionary, gratitude is a personality trait, a mood, and an emotion! And as an emotion, gratitude is a feeling of happiness that comes from a *realization of appreciation.* So when we are in a grateful mood, grateful emotions are more likely to be present. When we consciously choose to "be" grateful or to realize a sense of gratitude for something in our lives, or that has been offered, we are living in a much deeper sense of our spiritual nature, our Divine-Self.

According to Pierre Teilhard de Chardin, Jesuit priest and author of *The Phenomenon of Man, "Joy is the infallible sign of the presence of God",* also an outer expression of living in gratitude. Brene' Brown corroborates that in her book, *The Gifts of Perfection* in one of the findings that emerged from her research: *"...the people who described themselves as joyful all had one thing in common: an active gratitude practice."* She emphasizes that *"maintaining an 'attitude of gratitude' is insufficient to cultivate joy unless it translates to a behavior."* She said she was surprised that gratitude was experienced first, that is wasn't happiness that made us grateful, but gratefulness that made us happy. So a practice of gratitude, of intentionally seeking to appreciate what life offers, is necessary to align with our natural sense of joy as a sign of the 'presence of God" from within us. Gratitude is a sign healing is taking place and we have begun to realize a meaningful life once again. We are living in our authentic sense of self when we appreciate life and what it offers in every experience, whether we wanted it or not. As contradictory as it sounds, we can experience gratitude and a sense of joy in the midst of sadness and loss in life – because we choose to experience it.

I considered if there is a difference between feeling grateful and feeling gratitude? They can both be considered feelings, but slightly different at the same time. According to the Oxford Dictionary, the word "grateful" is defined as *"showing an appreciation of kindness."* Being "thankful" is a feeling, but being "grateful" is an action. Thus, "gratitude" is more than just the feeling of thankfulness, it is living in the awareness of it.

Does that mean gratitude can change our lives? I believe it can. Gratitude allows us to appreciate what we have rather than what we don't have – we see the good, what supports us, what makes a difference in blessing us rather than the opposing negative in our experiences. Gratitude can change our lives because it is the single most powerful source of appreciation that any of us can tap into, when we take the time to pay attention to the amazing beauty and miracle of life all around us. Gratitude is such a powerful force within us it is actually included in the Law of Attraction as another name for the Law of Prosperity, or as a law in and of itself: The Law of Gratitude. It is a spiritual law that supports our aligning with all that we desire, ask for, and deserve. The Law of Gratitude underlines that if you believe firmly that the Universe or God, the source of all life, depending on how you view it, is there to provide all that we want, ask for or imagine, and most importantly, that we deserve what we receive. When we live in a sense of gratitude, we attract more positive and prosperous manifestations into our lives. We relate to what we have and act in accordance to it. So seeking gratitude within even our most challenging experiences of life, especially when in the midst of pain and loss and the tragedies of life, we seek our healing and restoration to living a meaningful life.

The practice of gratitude becomes a way to shift our focus away from what either distracts us or causes us pain, and instead seek the things that bring a feeling of joy into the moment. It can be as simple as remembering to smile more often, to appreciate nature and the beauty around us, to breathe in the scent of a newly opened rose, or to tell those we love and appreciate that we love them. Take time to watch an inspirational movie or show or spend time with friends or someone we enjoy time with. Take time to nurture the relationships we have, realizing how important they are in life. And in a deeper practice, start a gratitude journal to write down something "I am grateful for" each day and reflect on it, maybe posting on your social media accounts each day to share with the world, adding value and vibration to what you claim. Be more intentional in what you notice around you and focus on the things that inspire you or bring a smile to your face. Shift away from the things that emotionally drain you or do not enhance your moment. These are simple things we can do for a lifetime, but especially while healing grief to support our moving forward in meaningful ways. For me, breathing was something I could be grateful for in my most challenging and pain filled moments. It made a difference.

Know that your willingness to enter into the process and practices offered in the pages of this book are building a stronger, more resilient spiritual foundation that will support you in more empowering ways in the future. And when any new pain from loss comes into your life experience potentially triggering grief once again, you will be prepared to activate the tools that support your healing from Day One. For grief is not a onetime experience in our lifetime. It comes in many ways and in many forms and can impact us on many levels of life existence. We experience loss everyday with the setting of the sun when we lose the light of that day, or when we have a flat tire or your child breaks your favorite cup. It is not just the big ones that trigger some form of grief. I still feel sadness every time I think about a favorite coffee table I had to sell when moving from one state to another because it would not fit either in my car to move it or in the space I was moving into. It was a practical thing to release, but I loved it and miss it every time I have moved again and realized I could have used it in the new place I live. This may seem silly, but the feeling of loss is real and I have to take a moment to process it when it comes up. I really loved that beautiful round marble-and-walnut coffee table! But I can now appreciate the value it brought into my life in the past, and see how that or something better will flow into my life as a replacement because I am grateful for its existence. And it has happened over and over again.

I have lost pets so beloved that when my mind reconnects with a memory of them or something triggers that memory, I feel the pang of sadness in my heart and have a little memorial in my mind for a moment. Especially with my first horse Alavan, my sweet half-Arabian/half-Quarter Horse who had to be put down after a pasture mate belonging to a friend kicked him in a hind leg, breaking it severely. It was a heart-wrenching experience for my eleven-year-old self. The same thing happens frequently with memories triggered around my son. I often see a young man who reminds me of him and long to hug him. I know that person would think I am a crazy lady if I really did it, but the thought passes through my mind. Or tears spring into my eyes. I yearn for him in that moment. You may have those little memory hits happen unexpectedly, too. Honor them when they happen, for they are the gift of loving deeply. Feel the gratitude that wells up for the cherished memory your heart holds forever as an infinite blessing. Smile when they come up.

During this writing I have had a sudden heartbreaking dose of grief activated with the news of our beloved eleven-and-a half-year-old dog, Morgan, a Beagle/Lab mix, being diagnosed with lymphoma. She has been given up to two months to live before we will need to make that extraordinarily difficult decision to let her go permanently. We are following the vet's advice of providing her palliative care for comfort, and our additional prescription for all the treats she wants as we enter these last few special months of time with her. We plan to spoil her and love her with all the attention we can roll into this short time, to let her know how special she is in our life. Morgan has always been healthy and energetic, so this unexpected news was a gut punch we didn't see coming. We spent the first few days of this news with tears flowing and emotions very raw as we come to grips with something we didn't think we would have to face for at least several more years.

Right now, we cannot imagine a day without her sweet face reminding us it's time to eat or go for a walk. Her cute little ways of getting our attention with a soft "woof" or knocking her water bowl around because it's empty, or ripping the stuffing out of her animal toys, or sneaking food off the coffee table when she thought we weren't looking. She is a full member of our family, and right now we do not know how we will be complete without her in it. It is beyond our ability to imagine, and yet we will have to experience loosing her way too soon. We do know we love her enough to release her from any pain when the time comes because any other decision would be cruel – as many of you have already had to experience as pet owners. It is an excruciating and loving choice in life that will provide yet another opportunity to learn from grief. This has been another example of how we cannot predict what circumstances life will throw at us or have any control in preventing from happening. We must embrace it and all the emotional pain it brings or allow it to destroy us. I am just beginning to consider the gift in this heartbreaking moment in time. I'm pretty sure it is about love.

A surprising gift that blessed me over and over the five years my husband Michael and I owned our Toyota Prius came when we went to the DMV to register our new car in downtown Cincinnati, Ohio, in 2015. As is the case, we were randomly given our new license plate: GTJ 1214. I nearly dropped it when I realized it stood for: **GoT Justin 12-14** – his birth date! The first time in my life I could remember my license plate number! I felt like he was driving with me every time I got in that car. We just recently had to release our Prius as it had served out its ability to be financially feasible, but kept the license plates. I was going to frame them to place somewhere special for me to always remember it was a sign Justin is with me everywhere and those plates were truly a blessing from the universe the day that plate number was assigned to our car! But I was delighted to find out we could transfer the plates to our new car, so Justin still rides with me wherever I drive, blessing me and our car mile after mile!

We never know when a surprise from the universe will come unexpectedly in a given moment. It is our job to recognize and claim it, a constant reminder that whatever we have lost in the physical is still a part of our lifetime as long as we are breathing. It may not be in the form we desire, but it is still a part of our lives and who we are. The feeling of gratitude for each blessing that enters our experience is a reminder that the universe is stacked in our favor. Gratitude automatically increases the vibrational frequency of our mind, body, and Spirit connection, aligning us with a jolt of wholeness as a result. Gratitude enhances our feelings of joy, expands our awareness of the world around us and magnifies everything we experience in positive ways. Gratitude can change us at our core. It certainly can transform grief, allowing us to move forward with a more meaningful sense of purpose and appreciation.

I have noticed in the years since Justin's death how I have been changed at depth. At the core I recognize I am not the person I was on June 7, 2013 when I received the call that Justin had been found dead. And maybe I don't want to be that person anymore. I have come to a place where I can appreciate who I have come to be. My profound experience of grief has transformed me into someone I like better, someone I can relate to more, and somewhere within I am happy to be expressing as. I am more courageous, more compassionate, but maybe a bit less tolerant. I say that because I have less tolerance for pettiness, for mean-spiritedness, for gossip, and judgmental behavior. Not that I am perfect and never enter into any of those behaviors myself, but I challenge myself to notice when I do and correct my words, actions, or behavior to someone I want to be, do or express, to one I can align with my divine nature more authentically. I notice I am more short-tempered and unwilling to waste my time with any of those things that do not support, uplift, or allow a positive outcome for everyone impacted in a situation. I now feel that my intolerance serves me, as my new me, in many ways. However, I do have to watch how it shows up, as intolerance can also create negative actions if I am not observing what is triggering my pull to react rather than respond. Getting caught up in intolerance can reduce my sense of mental well-being, therefore is not a healthy form of behavior when applied outside of authenticity. Noticing what is triggered within me is an opportunity to choose not to engage the emotions that come up in negative forms and share only what is positive, uplifting, and makes a difference in supportive ways. A big challenge for us all! I set the intention to practice each day to the best of my ability expressing gratitude, appreciation, and positive intentions.

That brings up watching the news and reading anything from the media. Can we tune out the negative and choose to find the truth at the core to discern how best to respond or even discern if it is ours to do anything? To the best of our ability, I suggest we do. It is my challenge, for it is so easy to get hooked. It is easy to have grief triggered from the news reports of how other people's lives have been impacted or what is happening in the world and the impact on people everywhere.

I notice I get triggered from reports every time I hear or see another mass shooting has happened. It is too close to my experience of the pain of loss, as a gun was involved in my son's murder. I feel the pain of the families involved, the horror, and the unbearable grief that is triggered in their very souls. The unexplained actions of someone who intentionally took lives without concern of how it will impact the lives of those touched by their act is beyond understanding. My suggestion is to not attempt to understand, as we cannot get into someone else's mind and relate to their choices. I know I would never think like that person, so my best plan of response is compassion and forgiveness. To open my heart to those affected, and forgive those who "know not what they do," as they are not acting from the awareness of their Divine Nature or they would not cause intentional harm, pain, or destruction to life in any form.

At this writing the world has found itself living in social distancing and isolation, with a majority of businesses closed and only what is considered essential in operation. I am observing the many forms of grief being triggered from the unique timing of everyone experiencing life as-we-know-it coming to a halt, perhaps changed forever. Many are losing loved ones from this Covid-19 virus, and all of us are affected from just hearing the numbers of the tens of thousands who have died and even more who are sick. Those who have not established grief skills or are unaware of tools to practice in support of this unexpected life-altering worldwide event, are struggling more than others. I see the great need for support for those needing help in how to manage the underlying emotions of grief being stirred. I am hoping to be able to reach out in more effective ways to offer that support through Face Book Live, virtual retreats and webinars. Being willing to speak to the very real emotional impact of grief in our human experience is needed more than ever, so I challenge you readers to step up where you can or share this book or other resources to support making a difference around us. But know whatever is happening, there are tremendous opportunities for us to reflect, observe, and take time to consider what we may be willing to change, create, or transform during this time. New ways of doing things are being born in this moment and wonderful new insights and discoveries will come to light. Yes, we may need to grieve what has changed or appears to be lost, but there has been much that needs to be changed and transformed to better serve humanity and the world around us. There will be much for which to be grateful, so take time to notice it.

Still, each day life can bring something that triggers sadness within me. I know I can be sitting with tears streaming down my face because something I just heard or watched touched that pain of memory when I first had to take in what had happened to my son. I feel the pain of those who are hearing for the first time what has happened to someone they love and the horror they are beginning to grasp. My heart cries out for them, for you, for our planet. Our souls will forever be touched by the pain and loss of life around us. It is part of our human experience, whether we want it or not. So how must we grieve? It is a learned practice to move through grief with grace and the willingness to find a way to discovering a new sense of meaning for life. My intention is to support you, to offer what I know, what I have learned, and that it is possible to live with it.

If you have been told to "get over" grief, it came from someone who did not understand that is not what we do. We never "get over it," but we do learn to live with it as who we now have become. Managing grief is a practice of a lifetime. We can get better at it in time; the triggers can become less intense in time. We can become more willing at allow tears to flow whenever they well up, as a reminder that we love deeply, and we can shift to our cherished memories with gratitude for their existence.

Gratitude is the natural result of transformational healing. According to Neale Donald Walsch, author of the *Conversations With God* books, gratitude is the natural expression of our Divine Nature and reminds us we are aligned with it in the depth of our soul. Gratitude is an uplifting flow of vibrational energy that ignites an aliveness within us that stimulates the creative flow of expression at a high level of manifestation. It is right up there with bliss, a sense of joy at our core.

One practice I learned from Neale Donald Walsch, and I encourage anyone to use daily, is to set an intention each night before you go into sleep to wake up with gratitude. Then, first thing in the morning before getting out of bed, allow your mind to think of gratitude, set a gratitude intention for your day. What am I grateful for today? Dwell on that for a moment to set the energy of your day. Even if you are reeling from internal pain and grief, it is possible to come up with something to be grateful for. In the early days after my son's death I would often think only, *"I am grateful I am breathing,"* and take a deep breath. Throughout the day I would check in with my breath to remind me it is my connection to life and to Godness, the divine energy active in and through me now! Sometimes it was *"I am grateful for feeling,"* as it meant I was shifting out of a numb state where I was not functioning in any state of awareness. So I could appreciate feeling, no matter what the feeling was. Maybe it is gratitude for having my morning coffee or tea, or having something to nourish my body. Or maybe just to have somewhere to go that day, a reason to get dressed. Or that I had the capacity to love deeply! There is always something to be grateful for that will elevate your vibrational energy to be more aligned with your divine wholeness and shift your reality in the moment.

The grief coaching program I graduated from is called Grief to Gratitude, as it is about a natural shift from pain to gain, from grief to realizing the gift within and being grateful in receiving it. Everything in life offers us a gift and something for which to be grateful, if we are willing to open ourselves up to what it is offering. In hindsight I can say I am grateful for every challenge that came into my life experience because I would not be who I am today without having walked through them. Would I want to re-experience them? Heck NO! But appreciate the gifts I realized because of what I went through? Heck YES!

I challenge each of you to begin to see the value of how you are enhanced by the pain from loss and the process of grief in your life. I know, a part of you may still be screaming within, I want _____ back! I don't want this now.... And yet, we cannot have back what we want, what we miss, what we grieve. That is denial of the facts, of the reality that what is gone can never be replaced in the form we knew and loved. It is painful to accept, but if we do not, we can never move forward with a meaningful intentional life. And that would be a tragedy in itself. I have learned to move forward, even living with the grief of my son's death every day. I am still learning to be comfortable with it, some days not as well as other days. It is a feeling I am getting familiar with as a new part of who I am. I have stopped attempting to rid myself of feeling grief triggers, as that just pulls me back into resistance and pain. The initial pain we experience is from resisting what has happened and rejecting it from our reality, something our mind cannot yet process. As we shift the energy around what we reject, we allow the healing process to begin and a new energy to call us forward rather than hold us back. We are still living; we must continue to play in this physical existence with all the rules, restrictions, and realities this human experience is about. So you decide how you will participate, what you will be, do, and create. It is always our choice even when we don't like the options ... so make new ones, better ones, more bold and profound ones, outside the box ones.

Each day we get to choose: what will I do and how will I show up? It is absolutely fine to decide today I will do self-care and not engage with others or go outside my home, but simply stay in and take naps between reading or watching movies and eating snacks (preferably body nourishing). It is all part of healing mind, body, and soul. Each day is part of a continuous stream of life experiences, choices, and responses that add to the manifestation of our reality.

What wants to come forth within you now? A great daily question to ask!

SELF-CARE: AN OUT PICTURING OF GRATITUDE

I think it is important to note that something gratitude can often inspire us to do in our unraveling of grief to embrace life process is to include self-care as an important element in our healing. Self-care is an important part of our health and wholeness for our spiritual growth and development in general, but is especially important when experiencing the impact of grief. During this time our bodies need more pure, nourishing, healthy food, body movement, and positive mental input than ever. Everything we feed our mind, body, and soul contributes to our physical, mental, emotional, spiritual, and social health and fitness. When we are processing the extreme energy of grief, the impact of what we feed our mind, body, and soul is even more important. What if I just ate junk food because it was easy and more pleasing? Does indulging in what I know is bad for me somehow make up for what I have lost? Does it truly make me feel better? No, our bodies are screaming for something to support it during this time when the fuel we take in is being used at a higher rate than normal. If I indulge in alcohol and drugs to stay numb, that becomes a form of resisting what has happened and leaves me in a place of sometime having to come out of the stupor and face the reality of what is now. Falling into addiction is perhaps an even more painful process when added to grief, and certainly not one that supports health and wholeness in grief.

I am not attempting to demean the reality of deep grief, but please be willing to love yourself enough to give your mind, body, and soul what it needs to thrive and support you in the healing process. Alive food supports aliveness. Positive loving thought supports vibrational alignment with wholeness. Physical exercise supports our body in maintaining strength, flexibility, and balance. And it all provides the energy needed to take positive action. Without those things we are crippled in our ability to heal and transform our experiences. One step at a time, consider what you need to be your best self, your strongest self, your most productive and nurturing self. Every choice contributes to the wholeness of our future existence. It actually is part of creating and living a prosperous life as well. Without a vitally alive mind and body we are out of alignment with the abundance of the universe and every other area of our lives. Grief interferes with this vitality and aliveness within. It is calling for our attention to love ourselves, especially in the midst of emotional pain. We all need an opportunity to practice self-love, and grief on all its many levels is one of the ways life provides us with that opportunity.

PRAyER IS A FORM OF GRATITUDE

I haven't said anything about prayer as yet. As a minister and spiritual educator who has spent twenty-five years teaching about prayer and the practice of prayer, I feel it would be relevant to share my thoughts around my personal belief and practice. My belief and understanding of true prayer is not in praying to a God or source outside of myself. When I offer exercises of guidance into a meditative process of breathing or listening or discerning what the voice within you offers, it is the same thing as practicing prayer to me, without naming it as such. Prayer is the action that takes us deep within ourselves to connect with the Divine, what I call Godness within us. The Divine is the vibration of life, the Source of life that we may call God, or by any other name, and when we align ourselves with that high-vibrational creative energy that activates wholeness through our act of prayer.

137

The Divine within is the absolute unchangeable essence of creativity that contains everything that exists in the Universe; anything that has or ever will exist as potential to be manifested into the physical reality. When we align with wholeness, the perfection of our Divine Self, we are healed in mind, body, and soul. In the act of prayer we are guided from the Wisdom of Source, the Godness within us, and we have all that we need to take intentional and empowering action to evoke change. Prayer allows *us* to be changed in mind and body, not to change the world around us. It is not about appealing to a God beyond us as worthy enough to receive what we want. It is not to change the mind of God to bend to what we want. We cannot change any circumstances in our lives without being willing to change the things that are in the way, blocking the way, or preventing the way of manifesting what we desire. And it starts with changing from within. Almost everything that is in our way requires a change in our thinking to allow a shift in the direction of what we want to be or experience. Prayer assists us in changing our thinking and opens our minds to the possibility of something new, perhaps beyond what we can conceive of in our personal limited consciousness. It can also connect us with a feeling of comfort, as in the mourning process of seeking a connection of God, our Source, and to know we are not alone and have all we need to manage the pain of life.

So my version of prayer is a part of my healing and transformational process of grief and any other experience of my life. It is a process of going within, releasing the active thoughts of my conscious mind and opening up to the unlimited wisdom of the Divine within – the Godness within me that knows better what to do than my personal limited human mind. I may have a question in my mind or desire for guidance around a specific thing, but the process is still about releasing active thoughts in my conscious mind and being open to new thoughts, ideas, concepts, or possibilities as the realization of Truth – the Wisdom of the Universe. I come back into my conscious mind with a new realization, understanding, and assurance of how to move forward or what action to take; and a realization of appreciation for whatever was received. For gratitude is always the result of communing with Spirit. Gratitude is the expression of the Godness within all Beings, a sign of that presence within us.

- **Prayer practice steps:**

1. Sitting in a comfortable position with outer distractions removed, close your eyes. Begin focusing on your breathing as a way to calm your mind. Following your breath for a few inhale and exhale flows, relax your body and mind.

2. Consciously release any negative thoughts, fears, doubts, and all mental distractions. Say within your mind something like this: *"I now intentionally release anything and everything that is a distraction to this moment. I consciously release anything and everything that prevents me from experiencing the wisdom and guidance of the Divine within me now!"* Focus on that thought to clear your mind.

3. Breathing in, now focus on a positive thought, affirmation or mantra. Something like: *"I am love,"* or *"I am peaceful,"* or *"I am now open and receptive to the abundance and wisdom of the God within me."*... Repeat that in your mind a few moments until the sense of your physical self begins to become less noticed.

4. State your desire – either within your mind or out loud to yourself. *"I am open to the wisdom within that knows what steps I need to take to realize my good, or abundance, or way through a challenge"*... Avoid pleading for help with a

problem, as that focuses on the problem and energetically asks to receive more of the same. Focus on the desired results rather than the problem; what form do you want to realize? *"I am open and receptive to the realization of a renewed and meaningful life" or "I am open and receptive to realizing the gift within my grief...."*

5. Sitting in an open receptive space, listen to what may come through to you to hear, experience, or feel, without expectation. Simply listen and if your mind wanders, shift back to your intention.

6. When it feels you are ready to end this prayer time, take a deep breath and consider what you have realized in the experience. Is there an "aha" or inspiration resulting from your time listening?

7. From that realization a natural expression of appreciation normally comes forth. Express appreciation for what you have received in your prayer time with a sense of gratitude. Say within you or out loud a statement of appreciating – something beyond "Thank you God." Make it deeper and more meaningful. *"I appreciate the gift received in this moment and move forward with a deep commitment to implement it into my life now." Or, "I am grateful for the blessings received."*

You have now experienced true active prayer. Use this practice daily to stay aligned with the creative energy of life moving in and through and as you in each breath you take, and to stay in the consciousness of gratitude and mental well-being as you are healing grief.

EXPERIENCE DIVINE LOVE SHIFT – TO-GRATITUDE MEDITATION:

A guided meditation to experience the Divine Love from within that naturally shifts us into gratitude for life. * *To listen to the audio link of the following meditation exercise go to website: www. unityawakeningways.org*

- Gently closing your outer eye and consciously allowing your inner eye of awareness to be noticing your experience.

- Bring your attention to your breath for a moment as you see your breath moving into your body, expanding into each cell of your being revitalized you with living giving vibrational energy and then as it flows back out with all that is no longer supporting your heal and wholeness lovingly removing those energetic elements that interfere with sustaining life.

- Just notice as an observer for a few breath cycles…how it relaxes your body and stills your mind when simply noticing…

- Now feel your breath and how it supports and energizes you…

- Bring your attention to your heart space…begin to feel your breath breathing through your heart…

- Feel you heart opening to experience the unconditional energy of life…

- Feel the unconditional love of the Divine Mother Within enfolding you with this love…accept it into your heart –let your mind realize you are receiving it…

- Imagine this feeling as a warm hug of love, comfort and nurturing energy…allow it be felt as deep and as meaningful as you possibly can…(Gong vibrations enhance)

141

- Know with the depth of your mind and the intelligence of your heart you are unconditionally loved and accepted by the divine mother within you with, the feminine energy of the divine source of all life, that which we call God. Continue to feel all that it is offering you…(feeling gong vibrations…)

- What is the feeling that is welling up within you now?

- Do you feel appreciation for the gift of love received in this moment?

- The gratitude that wells up when we realize the blessings of a gift received? Allow the feeling of gratitude to expand within you…(gong vibrations expand feeling)

- Acknowledge the gratitude for the gift of unconditional love from your Mother Within – affirm in your mind "*I am grateful for the unconditional love received, knowing it is always available to me in each moment!*"…(*repeat*)

- Internalize that gift of knowing…

- As we prepare to return to the physical moment with each other, intentionally accept the gift you have received and that you bring back into your daily moments of life with you…

- Being to feel your physical body, the place where you are seated and the essence of the room you are in…opening your eyes in gratitude and a renewed sense of appreciation for all the blessings offered as gifts of love from within.

- We simply say a heartfelt, *Blessed be.*

Take a moment to reflect on your experience and write down any realizations, thoughts and insights you wish to capture from this meditation.

"I still miss those I loved who are no longer with me but I find I am grateful for having loved them. The gratitude has finally conquered the loss."
~ Rita Mae Brown

CHAPTER 11

FINAL THOUGHTS ABOUT GRIEF AND ITS IMPACT ON THE WORLD

As I am writing this book, I am living in the emotions of my heart and what it is compelled to share with you. I ask myself, what would make a difference to anyone reading this book right now? Is there something more I have learned that I can share with you to support your grief process in this moment?

1. The first thing that comes to mind is to have gentle compassion for yourself every day. It is the best support I can suggest. Enter into that gentle loving place within you that is like a warm hug and reminds you there is love, guidance, and wisdom for you there. You are never alone even if it looks and feels like it. Allow the warmth of Spirit to envelop you like the loving hug of the mother that is within every being; the mother we yearn for in times of pain and loss. Connect with her and share all your pain, sadness, and sorrow. Imagine her receiving it as it is released from you, to comfort you, and bring you some peace. Surrender into that peace and bathe yourself in it. Experience it permeating

every cell of your being, relaxing and letting go of the intensity of your pain. With this new sense of peace, let go and rest. Imagine yourself slipping into a deep sleep, giving your heart and mind much needed recovery time. Know that when you awaken, you will feel comforted and ready to do whatever is next in your day. Give this gentle meditation to your body, mind, and heart whenever the pain takes over and you are in need of comfort, peace, and rest. Give yourself this gift as needed, spiritual doctor's order.

2. The next thing I would offer you is to give yourself permission to ask for help. Ask someone you trust and can feel safe and vulnerable with to support you. Seek someone to talk to you, listen to you, to cry with you, or feed you, someone to run errands for you. Whatever you need, have the courage to ask. There will be someone who would love to be that support for you. They may just be waiting for you to ask, not wanting to intrude. I know for myself that asking for help can be a huge growing edge, but now is the best time to take that leap. Would you do that for someone you cared for? Yes, most of us would, so do not begrudge someone the opportunity to serve and love you.

Asking for help can also involve seeking professional support. If it feels that processing grief is more than you can do alone and it is impacting your life in adverse ways, seek a professional therapist or grief group to give you that support until you can begin to take steps on your own.

Grief coaching can also be invaluable when you are ready to take those next steps into transforming the energy of grief and begin creating the meaningful life you would like to start manifesting. Once you begin to identify the gift within the grief you experience, you can begin the process of creating your living legacy. It is an empowering process that opens doors of awareness you may never have considered possible. It ultimately becomes more life coaching as you shift from the focus of pain to the focus of how you will live moving forward. That is when gratitude becomes evident as a result of the steps you have taken.

3. And very importantly, choose to begin to transform the pain from grief to embracing gratitude right now, today. Choose to be courageous, bold, and loving. Do you feel the call within you to heal, transform, and become the new and enhanced you that wants to emerge from grief? Are you ready to identify the gift offered and claim it? If you say yes, then reread this book, take in what serves you and use the exercises offered to take you into living life as a legacy gift to those who come after you, by intentionally making a difference and demonstrating it is possible to live a meaningful life because grief enhanced who you now are. And remember: thoughts of gratitude provide us with moments of grace and the time we need to move forward one step at a time.

4. One more thing, along the way, read others' grief stories of personal healing and transformation. Stories of others' grief journeys can be your inspiration to keep moving forward; to never give up on yourself, your heart, your mind, your soul's purpose to living this lifetime with meaning and intention. I am compiling some very inspiring stories to share in a follow-up book to be called: *"Unraveling Grief: Stories That Inspire Healing and Transformation."* If you have an inspirational story you would like to be considered in this new book, send me an email with the subject line: "Grief Stories Book" to: unravelinggrief@gmail.com

I often wonder what Justin would think about life now. What would he have changed, overcome, made of himself? Would he have overcome addiction and discovered what really made him happy? What would he be like in his 30's and beyond? Would his life perspective have changed? I know I will never have the answers to those questions in reality, but I think it is normal to wonder about someone we loved and had been a significant part of our lives, but are now gone from our physical world. To think, "I wonder what they would do about this?" Or would he have married and had more children? What would he have looked like as an older man? I think the questions and the wondering is a part of the healing process, too. For if we don't explore our thoughts, we shut down a part of us that is active and alive. When I spend time imagining, it allows me time to connect my heart with Justin's presence in my mind again, spending some special time with him. Sometimes I have a conversation there, too. It can feel like he is still with me, a comfort in my day. It may trigger some tears, but I can smile through them now. They don't bother me; they are a joy because I am feeling in the moment a very powerful gift I give to myself routinely, and for you to offer to yourselves as well. My little smiling boy who was born just in time for Christmas will always be my angel that inspires me, encourages me, and challenges me to be fearless, present, and aware in the moment of life happening. He will be my inspiration to be willing to step out of the boundaries of my comfort zone each day. The forever gift I now realize as a blessing within this human experience of grief.

CLOSURE:

STORY OF ONENESS

“An anthropologist proposed a game to children in an African tribe from the Xhosa culture. He put a basket full of fruit near a tree and told the children that whoever got there first won the sweet fruits. When he told them to run, they all took each other's hands and ran together, then sat together enjoying their treats.

“When he asked them why they had run like that when one could have had all the fruits for himself, they said, ‘UBUNTU, how can one of us be happy if all the other ones are sad?’”

‘UBUNTU’ in the Xhosa culture means: ‘*I am because we are*’ – the belief in a universal bond of sharing that connects all humanity.

I believe Ubuntu is a gift we can offer all beings everywhere as a way to love, honor, and support each other in the challenges, pain, and losses of life. We grieve in one form or another throughout our lifetimes. Why not honor the grief process as a way we can bond and join in Ubuntu to ease the way back into a meaningful life? Maybe in being the bit of *Kintsugi* that enhances the cracks within for each other, and the ‘golden resin’ that mends broken hearts and pierced souls from the most painful life experiences?

We could do better in allowing the experience of grief to be honored and supported as a very precious part of our human existence, something no one can escape or avoid. We could perhaps help to heal and pave the way for fewer broken people walking the planet acting out their pain, that in turn causes more pain and suffering in the world around them. I believe it is unresolved grief from the abuse and suffering of life that is being called to be healed and transformed in our world today. Our lack of recognizing the significance and importance of acknowledging the pain of grief in all forms has contributed to a world of people not recognizing the divine within each other, and therefore not realizing the impact their unresolved grief has on both their actions and every living thing on our planet.

What if we realized we are all connected in thought and mind, and with one collective breath we can align with each soul's wholeness? Imagine that in your mind; see a circle of beings holding hands around the planet and taking in a collective breath of oneness, and then we all exhale together into the peace of our connected hearts. What would we experience with each other then? Keep imagining it and one by one we all join together in mutual synchronized breathing. We could and can make a difference in a powerful healing and transformation of souls on our planet! I believe conscious breathing is the beginning and the catalyst of healing and a return to our wholeness.

Go back to the end of the Introduction of this book and practice breathing daily. We will all be on our way to a more meaningful experience of life, one breath at a time. And that allows us to enter into the process of unraveling grief as it comes, to heal and transform as we embrace the gift within our grief journey. The result is a meaningful life of gratitude and intentional purpose. It is something we all have available within us if we choose to accept it as a choice to live and believe deep within our souls it is possible.

Now one more thing: imagine as you consciously breathe as one in the spirit of Ubuntu, you reach out your hand into the infinite energy of Spirit and know there is a hand reaching out to you from the other side of existence to connect with you in the universal bond of unconditional love knowing together, *"I am because we are" connected in mind, body, and spirit for eternity, and we are truly blessed.* For me that hand is Justin's hand. Let the hand of your love reach out and connect with the hand you miss in this moment and affirm, *"I am because we are." And so it is!*

And as Marianne Williamson said, *"May all hearts be healed."*

Post Note: The author offers grief-healing retreats, as well as group and individual grief coaching online for those interested in her support and are ready to say, "Yes" to live again. Go to her website: www.unravelinggrief.com for Grief *Coaching Services, Online Course or Retreats* You can also email her coaching address: unravelinggrief@gmail.com to request more information. Meghan is also available to be scheduled as a speaker for groups and events, live or virtually, and for interviews in any forum, by going to *Contact Us* on the above website.

If you would like to share your grief healing story, please email: unravelinggrief@gmail.com to request a Grief Story Questionnaire to submit as consideration for publication in Meghan's next book: *Unraveling Grief: Stories of Hope and Inspiration.*

ABOUT THE AUTHOR

Reverend Meghan Smith Brooks, originally from the Northwest, is an ordained Unity minister having served ministries in Mesa, AZ, Brea and Pasadena, CA, Cincinnati, OH and currently in Tacoma, WA. After losing her son, she was called to enhance her ministry calling to become a certified grief coach, using her almost 30 years' experience in spiritual education, speaking, coaching and facilitating workshops and retreats. Along with her husband and partner, Reverend Michael Brooks, she is co-founder/spiritual director of alternative ministry Unity Awakening Ways. Meghan has produced 2-guided meditation CD's for healing and transformation. She now lives with her husband in Tacoma, WA. She has a surviving adult son and two granddaughters who bless her beyond measure!

For more information on her programs and services: www.unravelinggrief.com.